You Deserve to Sing

Thoughts and Questions

about the Value of Singing

for the Modern Human Being

Eva Cranstoun

Copyright © 2013 Eva Cranstoun

All rights reserved.

ISBN: 0615759572
ISBN-13: 978-0615759579

Dedication

I dedicate this book to my wonderful parents, *Elisabeth Swisher and Dr. Med. Johann Moravansky*, who gave me a childhood brimming with live music, nature and Waldorf education, and who graced me with their endless patience.

CONTENTS

	Acknowledgments	i
	Preface	Pg 8
	Introduction	Pg 17
1	A Silenced Society is in Danger of Losing an Essential Capacity	Pg 24
2	Thoughts About True Listening and Good Vibrations	Pg 37
3	The Three Realms of Being: Pathway of Manifestation	Pg 45
4	All the Parts of our Miraculous Vocal Instrument	Pg 50
5	What Healthy Singing Can Teach Us	Pg 80
6	Evolving Humanity Through Developing Musicianship	Pg 93
7	How to Get Started: Preliminary Exercises	Pg 108
	Conclusion	Pg 126
	Bibliography and Additional Recommended Reading	Pg 128

Acknowledgements

I want to thank my husband *William Cranstoun* and my three children for believing in me; I would like to express deep gratitude to my singing teacher *Christiaan Boele* (Germany/Finland), who introduced me to the School of Uncovering the Voice in a way that I was able to accept. Christiaan helped me put many of my puzzle pieces in order and always encouraged me to go even deeper. He officially certified me and has supported my work; a special thank you goes to my therapeutic singing instructor *Thomas Adam* (Germany/Swizerland), who trained and certified me as singing therapist and who showed me how to diagnose without judgment; many thanks go to *Ruth Hoffecker* and my mother *Elisabeth Swisher*, who lovingly dissected my first draft and gave me very useful, constructive feedback, *Dunja Popovic* for proof reading, and *Emma Lomax* for volunteering to be my editor and seeing me through to the end; Deep gratitude goes to my teacher *Michael Tamura*, who opened the world of subtle energy flow, universal joy and the reality of miracles for me, which added a whole new spiritual dimension to my singing, teaching, performing and observation; thanks to my daughter *Lara Trikha*, who gave me permission to use her picture on the front cover; and last but not least a huge thank you to all my *students*, children and adults alike, who have given me the opportunity to grow as a teacher and who have encouraged me to write this book.

Preface

I love to sing. I am also passionate about helping others to discover the love of singing, and through my years of working as a teacher I have been given the blessing and responsibility of knowing how to achieve this. I am certainly no scientist, mathematician, psychiatrist, physician or philosopher, but I understand the deep connection of these disciplines to my own fields of expertise: singing, music, parenting and Waldorf education.

Creation has given us everything we need through the countless miracles of nature, but also the responsibility of its stewardship. We have also been blessed, by the same source, with all the tools we need to heal ourselves, to make progress in our spiritual journeys and to become collectively more and more awake. To become true stewards of this planet we need to foster this inner growth.

I have found that the human voice is one of these essential 'tools' of human development. Its use and growth is dependent on the perfect interplay between all the other 'tools' and human capacities like Speech and Communication, Thinking, Feeling, Imagination, Listening, Awareness....

Discovering one's voice and musicality begins already in the very first years of our lives. I was lucky to have had a perfect foundation for developing an outstanding singing voice. Growing up in the 70s and 80s together with my older sister Imme, in a household of very young parents in Vienna, was a lively and culturally rich experience.

To some, the story of my childhood may sound unreal, like a story of times long past, no longer relevant. And yet, as I am writing this I am only 40 years old.

We wrote our homework by hand, in cursive, with fountain pens; we researched our schoolwork at libraries, in encyclopedias and by interviewing professionals; calculators were cutting-edge technology during my middle-school years; we traveled primarily by train; there were no cell-phones; instead, we always carried a few coins in our pockets and used public pay phones to call home; there were no PCs (except those clunky ones at fancy offices and banks), no internet, no I-pods, not even CDs at first; we had vinyl records, tapes and "Walkmans"; there was no TV in our home (although most people did have TV) and no video games to entertain us children; there was no Karaoke to help with the singing; cameras needed rolls of film and had manual lighting adjustments. And at our Waldorf school's events, like plays and public presentations, we had to project our voices to be heard without a microphone.

And yet I was seldom bored.

I do not remember a time in my life in which I did not know how to sing. And if my singing was ever inaccurate or rudimentary, my parents never told me so: I could always sing. We sang on car-rides, on camping trips, during kitchen-chores, for bedtime, for waking, for games and family entertainment; we sang on all the major holidays and all the days in between; we sang about Summer and Autumn, Winter and Spring and we sang about animals, love, work and magic; we sang about nonsense and danced to it; we sang for birthdays, funerals, weddings and baptisms. We sang at school, too. Not just in music class:

we sang to begin the day, for assemblies and celebrations, to remember math-sequences, to learn foreign languages and to acoustically illustrate our plays.

I remember wanting to learn how to sing in a round. I was probably four or five. My sister, who is almost two years older than me, was able to do it, while I was not. It puzzled me and frustrated me, since I so loved to listen to my mother and father singing rounds with my sister. I was determined to join in with them, so I practiced and pretty soon I got it. I now realize that I was unusually young to have mastered this, and once I knew how to do it, I never tired of it.

I am afraid my parents got in trouble more than once with the lady who lived downstairs from us in the apartment building, who complained about rhythmical stomping (I was dancing with my invisible friend Ellie) and nasty, repetitive toots and squeaks sounding through the open window (I was practicing my first songs on my pentatonic recorder). They patiently accepted the trouble and never asked me to stop. I am so grateful! A lot of my early childhood play must be counted as practicing and developing my musical skills, although I was never consciously aware of learning. I just enjoyed it and was completely absorbed in the activity, as are all children who are given their time and space to play and to create.

My mother was juggling a busy life, studying music at the "Musikhochschule Wien" [University for Music and Performing Arts, Vienna], and taking care of us two small children, while my father worked at a local hospital as a young physician. I remember my mother regularly practicing pieces on the piano and her silver-flute. Somehow, these are some of the strongest, fondest memories of my early childhood: the sound of her music as I fell asleep, as I woke up, as I played with my toys. Sometimes I sat on her lap and watched in awe how her fingers firmly flew over the keyboard and how this confusing jumble of black marks on a page could somehow help her remember the music. Many of the compositions she worked on during those early years will still touch and comfort me deeply today, whenever I hear them being performed.

I remember my utter confusion when I noticed consciously for the first time, someone who could not sing in tune. I was still a young girl, yet I was genuinely concerned and felt strongly that this person needed help. In my childish understanding I already knew then what I know now to be true: *that singing should be no less essential to someone than speaking or walking, or the ability to use one's hands.* I thought for sure one of the adults around me would notice this person's predicament and help out, however to my surprise, no one did, and so I grew up a little more that day.

Gradually, over the next few years, I began to understand that even though helping this person would indeed be very important, it is even more important never to break someone's joy of singing through criticism. I learned that through my own, painful experience.

I was known in my class as a good singer, though so were several others. One girl, in particular, had a very lovely voice. My teacher once made the mistake of asking the two of us to stand and sing the same song in front of the whole class: first her, then me. Then - and this is where the mistake comes in – he asked the class to describe the difference in our sound quality. They described our voices quite accurately: mine as more silvery, bright, hers as warmer, round and golden. Maybe there was even no judgment intended, and yet I felt exposed, criticized and humiliated. No one knew, of course, that I already had a very clear idea of what I wanted my voice to sound like: warm, round and golden! I was in fourth grade, probably only 10 years old. And no one knew that I had just been told by my most revered teacher and my friends that I simply did not have what it took to sound the way I so much wanted to.

From then on, I began to work on the sound of my voice and I listened out for warm, golden voices that were clear, strong yet effortless, without the irritating "jiggles" (tremolo). Thanks to my wonderful parents and my grandmother, I had the privilege to hear several such voices on the stages of Vienna. My grandmother, who was very actively involved in raising us, would take my sister and me to the opera, theater and classical concerts that took place in beautiful historic concert halls and elegant theaters. We had to take a nap on those days, dress in fine clothes, get our hair brushed and braided and then ride the street-cars and subway to the city center. In all those years I never lost the overwhelming feeling of awe and wonder when we entered the old, royal stone buildings with shiny marble columns, fine, red carpets, sparkling lights and the murmur of hundreds of voices.

One of those evenings I remember we went to see *Hänsel and Gretel* by Engelbert Humperdinck. We knew many of the songs already, so it was the hardest thing for me not to sing along – but I kept quiet, for at the same time I loved those full voices on the stage, the orchestra, the colors. The Witch was so evil, I was appalled! Her house moved on gigantic chicken-legs, that was very funny. And the Angels were so lovely, they brought tears to my eyes.

Throughout our childhood we went to see dozens of performances, some several times. A few of the musical shows were: *Die Zauberflöte (The Magic Flute), My Fair Lady, Die Fledermaus, Fidelio, Don Giovanni, The Fiddler on the Roof, Cats,* and *Die Entführung aus dem Serail (Il Seraglio).*

When it came to making music at home, we had this professional quality from the performing halls of Vienna to compare our music to. It was a standard set so high, it was almost impossible to reach. Still, we practiced and listened and experimented. It never occurred to me not to sing just because others were better than me. It never occurred to me, in the same way it would never occur to me not to swim because I was not an Olympic competitor or not to skip, turn cartwheels and run because I was no professional dancer.

We always had private music teachers as well as music instruction at school. My sister studied the violin and the piano, while I was instructed in the recorder at first – later in my early teenage years I added the piano for a while, lyre (a relatively recently developed harp-like instrument with 3 octaves of chromatic strings, held on the lap and played with both hands), guitar, oboe, and, at the age of 16, I began my formal voice-training in the classical lyric style that Vienna is so well known for. Trying on all these different instruments, I was searching for one that was just the right fit for me. The recorder seemed too easy as I reached my teenage-years (although I don't agree with that notion anymore) and I needed a change from baroque music; The guitar was too hard and it hurt my back so much that I frequently cried through my practice sessions; I found the oboe to be a little weird – although I did have fun playing in the school orchestra - and it eventually became clear that it did not complement my singing at all; The piano was easy enough and I loved my teacher – but I loved listening to my mother's and sister's playing so much more, and faltered when I had to endure my own, halting beginner's plunking. So I did not follow through. This I regret still now, as I struggle to re-learn at my age what I could have learned so much easier in my youth. I always compared myself with the best and therefore was always keenly aware of my shortcomings.

Many people over the years have encouraged me and commented on my unusually fast progress – but I discredited their support most of the time. I have always been my harshest critic. This, too, I regret. But there is no going back, and instead I am picking up now with new vigor what I could have done 25 years ago: sing for people every day. Open their hearts and ears and inspire them to sing with me.

I began to struggle with some questions, deep esoteric questions, as I experienced the process of vocal development as a teenager and young adult. For example:

*

How does the activity of singing influence our state of being on all levels, body, soul and spirit?

*

What I wanted to hear in other's singing voices and what I desired to provide for my listeners went far beyond mere entertainment or self-expression.

Although it took me many years to find just the right words to express my asking and searching, I began to gradually find answers through my work, training and research. I began finding evidence in my students' progress and in my own spiritual development: The spiritual dimension of singing which I had been looking for is indeed a valid and powerful tool for our inner growth.

Deep questions such as this one are the background for this book. I don't claim to have all the answers, but if you are willing to ponder these questions with me and to try out some possible answers, we are ready to go on this journey together.

I hope this little book will serve as a nudge toward further exploration and study for anyone wondering about the power of the human singing voice and the world of sound and music.

Over many years I have been searching and asking questions, continuously exploring new perspectives. There is always more to wonder about, and the learning never ends! Much research has already been done in this field, and many masters have shared their wisdom in their own books. Often, when I was younger, I found myself enthusiastically beginning to read one of these carefully written books, only to find that the lofty, philosophical or scientific eloquence of the authors quickly smothered my youthful, creative but sanguine interest. With this book I am hoping to keep my wording accessible to anyone, provided they are willing to go deeper into the world of the soul. I am a practical person, but I also don't mind having many questions without definite answers, especially when I'm convinced that there is no such thing as a definite answer. Be forewarned that some questions I am asking in this book may be questions of this nature.

Join me in exploring thoughts, questions and experiences concerning this powerful instrument we all possess. I hope you will find them intriguing enough to continue your research and study of singing, after you have enjoyed this book of shared experiences and loving encouragement.

Introduction

A Renewed Approach to an Ancient Art

Not too long ago, singing was a primary means in any society for spiritual expression, entertainment, mental focus or comfort. People sang along with their work in the fields, in their kitchens or on the road; people sang their stories, sang for each other at receptions, parties and for rituals. Singing was part of education and of politics; it was part of work and part of play, equally. It was understood that singing is a powerful tool used to connect to each other and to our core being, to invigorate, console and raise our spirits. Built into our amazing physical bodies, this perfect musical instrument is always available to us. What a gift!

And yet, our western culture has the tendency to forget about this gift. We have forgotten the vital importance of the fact that divine wisdom has equipped us with the most perfect musical instrument for a good reason. In our culture, singing has lost its vital role of social and spiritual connection – and too many people have never had the opportunity of singing presented to them. It has instead been left to professionals in the entertainment industry and is now considered a rare skill that potentially pays a lot of money. Furthermore, the ability to sing is too often misunderstood as being primarily a way of emotional self-expression that includes performing, dancing and exposing oneself in front of thousands. This performing mode is indeed not for everyone! But just as I like to run, move and dance even though I am not a Marathon runner, gymnast, Olympic track-racer or professional dancer, everyone can sing and enjoy singing, even though some may choose not to perform.

If we expose young children to live music and singing, they will learn it quickly and naturally. Singing with a group of children can demonstrate what singing could be for us, if we did not coerce this inherently social activity into a performing mode. And yet, more and more often, the public is introduced by popular media to yet another child who sings, as the media say, "like an angel". This always makes me a bit sad - not because what they say is wrong, but because they make it seem as if such voices were extremely rare. Although these children do indeed have lovely voices, they more importantly have influential adults behind them who have noticed the child's ability to entertain, to act and to be center stage. What remains to be seen is whether they can become healthy young adults despite the enormous pressure of public performances and fame.

In my many years as parent and music teacher I know for certain that thousands of children have angelic voices and considerable, amazing, natural musical skills. Far too many give up their angelic sound in exchange for the popular over-emotional, manipulated sound, as they struggle to become the kind of performers who fit into the expectations of the harsh and highly competitive entertainment industry.

What is it that makes us crave the sound of such "angelic" voices? What is it we recognize in this pure sound of confident children singing with their whole being? It touches the heart. It connects us to our core-being, to the essence which religious people would recognize as God. This is what such pure music – and singing in particular – can do: connect us to our spiritual essence. It is high time now to re-introduce the spiritual aspect of the human voice to our understanding of singing. It is time to recognize and harness its power to consciously support spiritual, emotional and social development. This is what a renewed approach to singing must do: develop the understanding and mastery of the voice with its full impact on our physical, emotional, social and spiritual life. Such an approach cannot be meant for a gifted few with angelic voices, but must be accessible to all. Not to mimic other popular voices, but to discover the value and potential of our own, unique voice, must be the focus of this approach.

*

At the very end of the 19th century a little girl was born in Sweden. Her name was Valborg Svärdström . She must have sung like those children I mentioned earlier – she moved the hearts of her friends and neighbors with her angelic voice and singing was her constant companion. But not until her teenage years did she take up formal vocal development lessons. She went on to become a successful young opera singer, celebrated throughout Europe - but not without also experiencing for the first time a new awkwardness and self-consciousness about her own singing. In her Introduction to her book *"Uncovering The Voice"* she describes how the formal training and public demands on her voice slowly eroded her joy of singing and compromised her range and flexibility more and more. Indeed, she eventually suffered severely paralyzed vocal chords and was forced to suddenly interrupt her work as performer. With the help of a good friend and colleague who encouraged her not to lose heart, she experimented with the sound that most reminded her of her old, uninhibited voice of childhood: the sound of -NG-. Eventually Valborg Werbeck-Svärdström was able to completely recover her voice and return to the stage after only a few months. Now she had discovered for herself a new, healthier voice but found it to have a new quality; a quality that did not seem to fit into her old roles on the opera stage. Over several years she struggled with the contradiction between her old approach and her new way of singing. This led her to develop a unique school, specializing in a renewed, holistic approach to singing. She called it: *The School of Uncovering the Voice.*

With the support of her husband and invaluable meetings with her mentor Rudolf Steiner, she was able to develop this new approach to the art of singing. This new school openly works with the esoteric and spiritual aspects of the art as well as the immense healing capacity of singing.

Realizing the power of song as healing entity and pedagogical tool in addition to the artistic, a new collaboration between her work and medical doctors as well as educators and therapists emerged, all of which had already been working with the impulses that had begun to grow out of Rudolf Steiner's vast, influential work.

Werbeck-Svärdström's work was highly intuitive and personal, all exercises given to her students were very well thought out, musically pleasing and challenging to both mind and body.

After reading her book "The School of Uncovering the Voice" one might wonder why it does not include any of these exercises? In her first chapter Werbeck-Svärdström writes:

"In the art of singing, the starting point for all teaching can only be the teacher's own ability; for right learning in singing is based essentially on the capacity of imitation. Important though correct doctrines are, theoretical didactics can only be of secondary importance. As was mentioned in the beginning, the first task, and at the same time the task of the most all-encompassing importance for the developing singer, is to master the art of true listening, the development of the inner ear...."

This quote might shed some light on her decision not to give written instruction for practical exercises, which would have posed a serious danger of being frequently misinterpreted and might have unintended effects on the reader's voice. Werbeck realized that the most important element to be developed first and foremost is the *art of true listening*. This cannot be taught through written pages, but only through direct interaction with the teacher. Instead of publishing specific exercises, she decided to thoroughly describe her principles, experience and knowledge of the subject, so that it can be incorporated by students and teachers alike in their individual application.

   Exercises were passed down from teacher to student. Many of the exercises she developed for her students were uniquely designed for specific, personal issues her students faced. Therefore her "method" may have been experienced quite differently by different people. Fortunately for us, she was a meticulous recorder of her own work, and so a great number of the exercises have been preserved by her successors in her original, neat handwriting.

To anyone interested in her principles, thoughts and esoteric findings, I strongly recommend reading her book; but those who would rather begin their exploration by experiencing first-hand the rewarding and transforming process of this schooling, I urge to find a certified teacher who is thoroughly trained in this approach.

Here are some of the questions that led me to study the *School of Uncovering the Voice* and which brought up more and more questions, the further I continued down my path of vocal and esoteric exploration:

*

How important is it for an evolving human being to be able to sing?

What are we really expressing when we sing?

What does "True Listening" really require?

Why do more and more people claim that they cannot sing?

Could we imagine that we are simply offering our physical instrument as the means of manifestation for the spiritual entity we call music?

How can we begin to understand the psychological and spiritual dimensions of music and singing?

Why is it that we love to hear effortless, "angelic" voices?

Why is it that we feel revived, organized, validated and healed through a universally beautiful voice?

How can we achieve a voice quality that is as effortless and universally beautiful as possible?

*

My work as singer, teacher and therapist has led me deeply into these and many more questions, and there is always more to discover.

Join me as I make an effort with this book to organize and express on paper my many thoughts, questions and images around the complex world of singing and music, in connection with our continuous task of becoming better, more evolved human beings.

I have shared many of these thoughts, imaginations and questions with hundreds of students over the years. Repeatedly, supportive people have urged me to write them down, so here is my humble attempt to finally do so.

Chapter One

A Silenced Society Saturated with Noise is in Danger of Losing an Essential Capacity

Following Werbeck-Svärdström's statement about the primary importance of the art of True Listening, we cannot help but ask: How exactly does that relate to singing, to making sounds? Why does she place the listening as the most important pre-requisite for a good singing voice? I am sure you will agree with me when I say that good listening has everything to do with focus, attention and consciousness: Truly listening to someone or something means to give it our full, conscious attention; It means being able to process and understand what we hear. Listening and understanding like that requires the inner ability to find a quiet mind. And yet, to find a quiet mind is almost impossible to the untrained listener, if we are exposed to a constant onslaught of distractions. There is so much noise, images, movements, and information in our modern world to distract us! Clearly, our capacity to become good singers is under threat, if Werbeck-Svärdström's statement is true.

*

How can we create an environment that supports the development of true listening?

*

Have you ever been in a place where no sounds, other than the gentle rushing wind through the treetops, were filling the absolute silence? Where a hovering hummingbird or a cricket in the grass is the loudest sound in your environment? Have you ever been in a place where not a single electric appliance, buzz of distant traffic, overhead airplanes or entertainment media infiltrates your hearing? If your answer is no, go there! Find such a place – high in the mountains, or out in the desert. The impact on your senses is immense. Once you find such a place, listen; then add your own voice, and notice how you add your own voice to such majestic silence. You might learn a lot about yourself that day, about the way you meet the world, the way you place yourself and your voice into the world. Not too long ago most people knew about this kind of silence. They knew about total darkness too, but that's another story.

Years ago the bustle of a marketplace, with horses and carts, livestock, town-musicians, merchants shouting, people bargaining and arguing was just about the noisiest place anyone could imagine. But it always had an end to it too. People closed their stalls, stabled their horses and packed up their instruments - and silence came. The loudest sounds may have been the wind, a crackling fire, a horse in the barn, an owl in the woods. Now think about what a state-fair is like today. There is everything as mentioned before, but added to it are sounds of the modern day machines, electronic music, air conditioners, loudspeakers, cell-phone rings, amusement rides, traffic sounds. Even after everyone has left at night it won't be quiet, and it won't be completely dark. The hum of the emergency lights is ever present like a swarm of mosquitoes, the nearby traffic never stops, and airplanes and helicopters frequently fly overhead. When people go home after a long day at work, they often do not come home to refreshing and replenishing silence. They choose instead to be greeted by a large TV set that has been given central stage in their home life. Home appliances rumble, telephones ring, sirens rush through the neighborhood, stereos pound the very foundations of buildings, people argue, motorcycles roar, i-pods entertain 24-7...

Realizing the overload of noise in our daily lives, we may be faced with a few more questions concerning the challenge of true listening in our modern environment:

*

How do you add your voice to that cacophony?
How do you meet this onslaught of noise, how to you place yourself, your voice, into such a world?
How can we possibly make a difference?
Would it not be better to remain silent rather than adding yet more noise to the world?
And isn't it true that, since we do at times need to somehow cut through the muck of noise, we feel inadequately equipped without a microphone and some speakers, especially if we need to address a large crowd?

*

For thousands of years, public speakers projected their words without amplifications other than the natural acoustics of a large hall or plaza. Not only were they well trained to master the art of public speaking and performing, but the audiences also knew how to listen! Our ears have lost their sensitivity today, because unlike our eyes, we cannot close them. We cannot shut out the constant attack of "sound-tsunamis," even earplugs will not provide true silence. So our ears have begun to resign. We still hear, we have our physical organs and we cannot help but use them, but our hearing is not as sensitive, and we don't actively listen much anymore. Anything we need to actually pay attention to with our listening is usually somehow amplified. An alarming percentage of teenagers already show the typical signs of hearing loss we thought was reserved to the elderly. (You can find an abundance of studies and articles about this in libraries and on-line).

*

What happens within ourselves to all the sounds we cannot pay attention to?

*

Let's take a moment to introduce some thoughts about how sound is processed by our physical system. This is commonly referred to as "auditory processing".

Sound is received through our ears and "digested" by a number of systems in our organism. Every sound is heard, not just the ones that make it all the way to our consciousness. The thinking part of us will give the sounds a *label* if possible: associative processes link sounds to previous experiences. This association allows us to attach a concept, a name to it – a label. The sound we hear might also, through mere association with previous experiences, trigger an emotional response. The larynx will respond with miniscule but measurable motion to reflect the sounds. If we could be aware of *all* the sounds we take in and were able to properly analyze each one, "digest" it, we might be much more in control of the associative thinking and feeling that is moving through us constantly. But we're not aware of all of them – and so many sounds will enter our subconscious, triggering thoughts and feelings we have little control over. Those thoughts and feelings without apparent trigger or reason often seem the most persistent, cluttering our minds and muddying up our emotional well-being. (This, once again, can also be applied to visual input or smell, but just as earlier in this chapter, this is another story).

This issue reminds me of my cell-biology lessons in high school, where we learned about enzymes being responsible for digesting foods: when certain enzymes responsible for breaking down specific foods are not present in the digestive tract, the body cannot break down and use the foods. These foods will instead either be forced to circulate our system as toxins, be stored as useless fats, or else be eliminated in their original structure, leaving the body still hungry for nutrients. We can understand a lot about *sound processing* by looking at our digestive system. Let's once again compare sound intake with food intake for a moment.

Sounds are taken in through the intricate system of our inner ear and processed in our brain, just like foods are taken into our digestive system and processed. We then attach the sounds to concepts if we can, we label them, associate them with other sounds we might have heard before or create connections to feelings. Similarly, enzymes attach themselves to the food to analyze and break-down the food into more differentiated elements. Well processed sounds are consciously recognized, and with this understanding can reach a point of true silence in the mind; similarly, digested foods will leave our body nourished and with no ailments or residues. The physiological process in the cochlea demonstrates this silence very well: the sounds, once translated into a movement of fluid that stimulates very fine nerve endings, gets to a still-point at the end of the snail shell-shaped cochlea in the inner ear.

You can close your mouth and stop eating, you can close your eyes and stop looking; but it's hard to shut out sounds! Whatever sounds we cannot properly process (because there are too many, or we have no concepts for them) will either be ignored and stay in the sub-conscious realm, or else will remain in our mind to scatter our attention and get in the way of proper sound-processing. Those unprocessed sounds are there, floating around in our minds as chaotic memories, chattering away and littering our field of thoughts.

I see many children in the classroom having the hardest time finding a state of true quiet. It seems that those unprocessed sounds are constantly causing these children to talk, mutter, hum, drum and click to themselves, as if the overflow of unconscious sound-flotsam simply cannot be contained.

It is well understood that we become overweight and may suffer from a number of health issues from eating too much unhealthy food. We must consider the consequences of too much unhealthy sound!

We seem convinced that we need a lot of amplification. Even gatherings in fairly small rooms very often use microphones, although any speaker would be heard perfectly in such a space if the audience in the room was quietly listening. Even churches with great acoustics have elaborate sound systems set up, although the room itself amplifies sounds perfectly.

It appears that both the techniques of presentation as well as the auditory processing capacities are severely compromised in our society. Thus we attempt to make up for the lacking faculties with sound-amplifying electronic devices, creating an environment that further incapacitates our sense of hearing through overload and actual physical injury to the inner ear.

The loudness level of sound is measured in Decibel (dB). This is a logarithmic scale, like the Richter-scale measuring earthquakes. That means that with every 20dB increase, the sound is 10 times louder: 20 dB is 10 times louder than 0 dB; 40dB is 10 times louder than 20dB; 95 dB is 10 times louder than 75dB; 120 dB is 10 times louder than 100dB etc.

At various social events and venues, the music often dominates the setting by sheer volume. As we strain our voices to compete with the music, I wonder: why is it considered entertaining, good, needed, to crank up the volume past 85 dB? Aside from the complete eradication of normal conversation at such events, we should be amazed that no one has sued yet for bodily injury at clubs, rock concerts, dances and parties!

The United States Environmental Protection Agency (EPA) reports in detail on the harmful effects of noise pollution and provides a list of good resources for the public to educate themselves and the children on how to protect their hearing. Please take a moment to learn more at:

www.epa.gov/air/noise.html

Below I have configured a decibel chart, combining the standard chart from the EPA site with a number of other sources, of which the most useful and thoroughly researched one was the decibel loudness chart by Galen Carol audio:

www.gcaudio.com/resources/howtos/loudness.html

The hundreds of decibel charts and articles available do not always match up exactly, but that is understandable, considering that there is always quite a range of loudness possible on each example, depending on the distance to the measuring device and the specific source of sound.

Normal Noise levels, 0 dB to about 60 dB, are not harmful.

Very Loud Noise levels (70 dB to 85 dB) are not harmful but can become irritating and distracting and may interfere with our ability to focus. The threshold to potential damage through prolonged exposure is at 85 dB

Extremely Loud Noise levels (90 dB to 110 dB) are likely to cause gradual hearing loss if we are exposed frequently or longer than a certain length of time.

Dangerous Levels (115 dB to 190 dB) will cause hearing loss after fairly short exposure, or instantly, at 160 dB and above. The physical pain threshold is at 125 dB.

Dangerous levels:

- 180 dB = rocket launch; **death of hearing tissue**
- 165 dB = 12-gauge shotgun; **instant hearing loss**
- 150 dB = rock concert peak; firearms
- 140 dB = drag racing event; firecrackers
- 130 dB = jet engine (from 100 feet)
- 125 dB = **pain threshold**; jackhammer; indoor sports event
- 120 dB = amplified rock music at 4-6 ft.; car stereo; Symphonic music peak;
- 120 dB = rock concert, night club, ambulance siren
- 115 dB = leaf blower; chain saw; iPods (at maximum) movie theater peak levels

Extremely loud:

- 105 dB = helicopter; movie theater; tympani, trombone
- 100 dB = pneumatic drill; night clubs; French horn
- 95 dB = smaller motorcycle; silver flute, cello
- 90 dB = lawnmower, truck traffic, subway; noisy toys
- 96 dB = noisy restaurants; fortissimo piano

Very loud:

- 85 dB = busy city traffic; PE class at school **prolonged exposure can cause hearing loss**
- 80 dB = alarm clock; chamber music;
- 70 dB = vacuum cleaner; fortissimo singer; normal piano; air conditioner;

Normal levels:

- 60 dB = normal conversation;
- 35 dB = whispered voice
- 10 dB = breathing
- 0 dB = softest audible sound

Research has proven that exposure to moderate decibel levels of just over 85 for a prolonged period of time will most likely lead to gradual hearing loss. We can safely assume that we are exposed to 85dB or higher in noisy restaurants, in living rooms with large surround-sound TV sets, in bars and movie theaters and especially at in-door sports. It frequently strikes me as disturbing that so many people choose to bring their infants to such sports-events without ear-protection! These babies are being exposed to harmful levels of noise that has been proven to cause hearing loss, which will potentially lead to auditory processing problems and behavioral issues. Any noise marked as "dangerous levels" (115dB and above) on our chart should in my opinion be considered bodily injury: hearing loss is a serious problem and usually irreversible! Because of these considerations, I would start the list of "dangerous levels" farther down, at 100 decibel.

NIOSH (National Institute for Occupational Health) lists levels of permissible noise levels at the work place:

Unsafe Levels of Exposure:

- **110 decibels or louder**: regular exposure of more than one minute risks permanent hearing loss.
- **100 decibels:** No more than 15 minutes of unprotected exposure is recommended.
- **85 decibels:** Prolonged exposure (more than 8 hours) to any noise above 85 decibels is likely to cause gradual hearing loss.

Comparing these unsafe levels to the previous chart, this can explain why more and more teenagers are suffering degrees of permanent hearing loss that used to be reserved for the elderly only a couple of decades ago.

*

When did we start getting so loud and why?

Why is this high decibel level so important that we risk permanent injury to our delicate hearing organs?

*

   Looking at the modern world of music, this principle of competitive sound levels has created a dilemma: popular music has largely become entertainment that requires no particular listening skills because of its repetitive and fairly simple composition patterns and its sheer volume. People have music running all the time and simply talk over it a little louder!
   As we all know, in clubs, at parties, fairs and rock concerts, conversation is severely compromised for the benefit of non-verbal socializing and basking in radically amplified sound, unless you are willing to yell at someone in a conversation. So the threat of injury through dangerous decibel levels is not only to the ears but also to the vocal chords!
   It is indeed a wonderful feeling to have music loud enough to fill you up all the way into the bones, especially if you have no need for any form of communication. I enjoy that, too! But a full orchestra without any amps can do that for you; as can a trained singer with a piano or a few instruments or a good drumming performance. But such music not only fills us up acoustically but also requires us to give it our full attention, our active listening. Such music will never retain high volume over more than a couple of minutes, because dynamics are a vital part of a balanced musical experience.
   I'm sure you have observed that when you hear a cacophony of sounds, the loudest one will most likely get your attention.
   Have you ever noticed how the advertisements on TV and Radio are significantly louder than the regular programming? Those who create and broadcast these commercials know you are taking a break – getting a drink, running to the bathroom – they are

making sure you can still hear them! We have in a way become numb to sound-inputs, because there are simply too many to process. Our hearing instinctively becomes selective: Any sounds louder than the rest of the environment, will force their way up to the top of our mind's priority list. Following this human instinctive selection process, advertisers amplify the information they want us to hear. We don't have to actively listen at all: we are not given the choice. The message will come into our mind through sheer volume; it becomes dominant over our human conversations.

I have often noticed that children, who grow up in homes where the TV is always running, will involuntarily recite commercial slogans and jingles perfectly, but have difficulty maintaining and remembering a conversation. They also tend to speak very loudly.

Most of us usually shut down our auditory processing of the sounds around us to some degree, but advertisers make up for our lack of attention in sheer volume. It is not always easy to shut sounds out of our consciousness simply by ignoring them, and the louder they are, the harder they are to ignore. And so, reluctantly, our subconscious still hears, still processes and stores the information, the desires and "needs" the advertisers want us to have. And somehow, the more we resist this onslaught of advertisements and sounds, the more insistently they worm their way into our subconscious.

In fact, I am convinced that advertisers are not really interested in having our full attention. On the contrary, if we paid full attention, we would also have the ability to think clearly and make independent decisions about what we hear and see. A lot of modern advertising is indeed designed to appeal to our dream-like, subconscious desires, bypassing our discerning, conscious mind.

*

How can we cultivate discernment and attentive Listening, without becoming overwhelmed by so much sound input?

*

How many of us can still hear - and get irritated by - the constant high-pitched tone of a TV set? Who notices the refrigerator humming? I notice it now, as I'm writing about it. And I will notice with relief the new quiet, the moment it stops. I notice the hum of the computer, too. And it irritates me immensely, now that I pay attention to it, resenting and resisting it. But then I think gratefully of all the wonderful privileges these appliances provide for me: I give them space and purpose to be, and the irritation lessens. I can work again. I have reclaimed my own space and given the appliances theirs.

As a young mother I had to learn this lesson fast: when I really give my child my full attention, I am providing valuable space for her to be. I am validating her existence and honoring it by sharing time. Then the child learns by watching me, how to give other people space to be and time to breathe. When I manage to give space to my children, their voices, their creative minds, their listening – they will give me space to be in turn, and I can complete my tasks. I have, for that reason, followed my parent's example of not inviting any TV programming into my home until my children were well into their teens. Even now it is extremely limited. No uninvited TV advertising or programming invades my family's space and we are free to share good conversation with each other and to focus on our tasks at hand. There is enough invasive technology, even without the TV constantly running.

We all have become so used to being interrupted: the children need us to hear them, see them, to notice them! But the phones ring constantly; the radio blares; the neighbor's leaf-blower is in action again; in so many homes dinners are cut short because the favorite show is starting; the school or work schedule does not allow more than 10 minutes for lunch... And so the children learn that interrupting is their only chance to be heard. How many of us are such children, all grown up, and still our souls are begging to be heard and noticed? We continue to interrupt, in the hopes of getting some validation. I have had numerous friends like this, who ached for love and friendship, but still pushed people out of their lives by their agonizing habit of interrupting: no one ever taught them how to listen, how to find quiet in their minds, how to honor someone else's space and time, or in fact, their own space and time.

Being able to become quiet, slow down and cultivate our attentive listening mode in order to balance our fast-paced, noisy world is essential for your ability to discern and honor our own, as well as other people's time and space. It is indeed essential for our capacity to be aware of one another and to communicate.

> *We realize now that with the overload of sound comes the loss of an essential skill: Listening.*
>
> *And with the loss of the skill of listening comes the disappearance of an invaluable asset: the art of conversation and communication. We must realize that in this "new age of global communication" we are rapidly losing the basic ability to communicate well!*
>
> *Then, with the loss of communication skills, we become ironically isolated from one another as we intrude tactlessly and ruthlessly into each other's soul space.*
>
> *And without the awareness of another's space, without the ability to truly communicate, we forfeit one of our primary tools for awakening as a whole of humanity on this planet.*

Chapter Two

Thoughts about True Listening and Good Vibrations

As we have just explored in the previous chapter, there are significant differences in our capacity to process sound, depending on the level of attention it is given. If we listen without the attention – if the sound is mere background filler – a large percentage of it escapes our notice altogether. But if we listen with active attention, we notice a whole world of more detail, more nuance. The degree of our ability to do this *active listening* determines to a great extent our ability to create quality music, as well as our ability to hold sensible, constructive conversations. *Active Listening* begins with a focused mind and a functioning sense of hearing, but it also requires cultivating our awareness of another human being. It requires validating the other and giving the other being space to be, while holding and owning our own. Now you might say:

*

How does creating quality music have anything to do with awareness of another human being?

*

Any good musician will be able to tell you: no good music is really complete without a listener, an audience. The musician needs to "listen" to the audience's moods and energies and then respond accordingly. A good musician "listens" the music into being. A good audience can help significantly with this process with its own attentive listening, adding an aspect of community and communication. Even when practicing music all by oneself, once the music is truly flowing creatively, one does not feel alone anymore: the musician has caught the universe's attention and the whole world listens!

Everything in this world is in vibration at various frequencies. Vibrations are resonating with, disturbing or amplifying other vibrations. Our cells and fluids are little universes in harmonic vibration. When it comes to the material world, we know from our physics classes all about oscillating molecules and atoms, sound waves, heat waves, electric waves, light vibrations and even brainwaves that change their patterns and frequencies, depending on our state of consciousness and emotional condition. In the social realm we talk about vibrations as well, we might call them moods or "vibes" of different people, locations, situations or gatherings. We are using a term from the realm of science, effortlessly and without question, to describe accurately a phenomenon from the realm of soul. However, talking in detail about different levels of vibration in the soul of a human being and in the world of spirit is still a new idea to many, though it is really quite simple. The laws of physics apply to the realm of soul the same way they apply to the material world. When we compare the laws of frequencies of different substances in the material world, the picture becomes clearer: The lower (slower) the frequency, the more solid or cold the substance, the higher (faster) the frequency the thinner, but also warmer the substance. Physics explains this phenomenon with the frequencies of the molecules of substances as well as with the sound and light spectrums; each substance each color, each tone has its own unique vibration.

We can translate this to the spectrum of emotional states. In Chapter 22 of their book *"Ask and It Is Given",* Esther and Jerry Hicks offer a scale of frequencies for our emotions and suggest that in order to reach the top we must journey through the various frequencies on this scale. Low-frequency emotions that immobilize us are on the lowest level: for example, depression/lethargy/grief; anger, which moves us quite a bit more, is therefore on a somewhat higher frequency. The highest level is pure spirit, but as long as we are in a human body we are compromised there. But pure joyful bliss/love will get us as close as we can get to the highest vibration. A question once again arises for me as I study these phenomena:

*

Is it possible to influence and control the sound quality and range of my voice by adjusting my physical and emotional frequency? If so, how is it done?

*

We can explore this question from a few different angles.
  First, let's look at the wonderful physics experiments performed with tuning forks. Do you remember that? The vibration of one tuning fork will cause the others to sound with it if their frequencies are compatible, even if they are not directly hit. They can also cancel each other out, if their vibrations don't match. We are a bit like that, too. Except that our organism's and our soul's vibrations are not canceled out if they do not match, but instead they can shift (if we allow them) to match our environment.
  Johnathan Goldman (director of *Sound Healers Association* and president of *Spirit Music*) writes about this in more detail in his wonderful book *'Healing Sounds; the Power of Harmonics'* (Healing Art Press). He calls this process of aligning unmatched rhythms and frequencies *'entrainment'*:

> *"The different rhythms of the body may also be changed through sound. This is known as 'entrainment' and involves the ability of the more powerful rhythmic vibrations of one object to change the less powerful rhythmic vibrations of another object and cause them to synchronize their rhythms with the first object. Through sound it is possible to change the rhythms of our brainwaves, as well as our heart beat and respiration"* (Chapter 1, pg.14)

The creators of advertisements and movies know about this principle of *entrainment* very well and use it to influence our vibration according to their agenda. Their choices of music are anything but random. They ask themselves: "What do I want my audience to feel? Apprehensive? Scared? Romantic? Care free? Angry? Needy? Silly? Rebellious? Relaxed? Awake? Analytical?" And then they choose the genre of music that conveys the desired kind of emotional pattern. You might also notice that movie soundtracks usually give you the "soul-setting" before the actual corresponding event happens in the movie.

In addition to the emotional content of the music there is always also the intent of the artist, the content of his thoughts and the level of his consciousness, that determine to a great extent the influence his music has on the listener. Goldman says:*" Sound is a carrier wave of consciousness"*, meaning that, for example, I can sing you a sweet song, but if I as the performer don't have my intention, my mind, focused on you and the music but maybe instead I am preoccupied with being angry or irritated with something unrelated, then you might start resonating with my irritation and anger, because my sound carries it to you. On the other hand, if my intent is on healing, on communicating the spirit of the music's own intention instead of my own, your reception will be very different and can become a most powerful experience, even with the simplest of lullabies. Goldmann speaks about this state of being:

"It is that aspect of consciousness that is able to align with the sacred energy of sound. It is 'Thy will' not 'my will'. When we have reached this level, our intent is to become a vehicle of sacred sound and we are able to bypass the lesser aspects of self which may be out of balance" (chapter 1, pg. 19)

You will find this idea will come around a few more times.

Now let's look at these phenomena of entrainment and resonance in terms of our musical preferences and choices:

The artist expresses a certain state of being, an intent with a certain type of composition and performance. Whoever already lives in this mode will feel attracted to this music, because its vibrations are matching their own. People who function on a different emotional frequency level will not immediately feel attracted – they might even feel irritated or repelled. But the listener's soul-vibrations will eventually respond through the phenomenon of entrainment and begin to match the music. As an example: in my experience, the benefit of certain Hard Rock or Heavy Metal music is just like the punching bag at the gym: it releases and expresses emotional frequencies of rebellion, aggression, anger or of primal forces like sexual desire. Very therapeutic, this punching bag! But once you are done punching, you need to move on by maybe taking a walk or a bath, by reflecting, re-organizing, forgiving and so on. So in other words, there comes a time when you're not feeling aggressive and angry anymore. You're all punched-out! A different kind of music, a different kind of activity would much better match your state and promote your moving towards balance and inner progress.

But what if you now continue to listen to or produce this

particular type of music? The music is so powerful, it will re-create the state of aggression or anger in you through entrainment. A vicious cycle begins, unless there is a healthy balance provided.

I don't get angry very often at all. But when I do, I feel absolutely miserable. My stomach aches and my throat constricts and my heart burns. I need to move out of that state of being as soon as I can, because it is such an unbearable place to be in. I need to find balance.

Look at the majority of our modern rock artists. They are often undoubtedly ingenious, highly creative yet tortured beings, because they artificially keep their souls on the particular soul frequency of their music. Without seeking balance, they will become emotionally and physically ill. To ease their misery, many resort to taking drugs or to heavy drinking. Then they make some more aggressive music, and then they need more drugs.

I have never met a classical musician with a serious drug or alcohol problem. I know they do exist, but at a tiny percentage compared to the numbers coming from other genres of music. Why is that? Music from the classical tradition has, as one of the key features, a balance of moods built into its compositions: there are fast and slow movements, minor (introvert) or major (extrovert) moods and dynamic variation. It has the capacity to express the full spectrum of soul vibrations: Balance is built into the art form.

Do you see what is happening? Since the styles of music have specialized and fragmented more and more in our modern age, the element of balance is disappearing, and we have chosen to potentially limit ourselves to a much smaller range of soul vibration. Please understand that this is not only problematic for the musicians themselves, but also for their frequent listeners.

Another style of music that has become popular recently, is a pop-style created and performed by some very young artists. This very simplistic and highly digitized style expresses out-of-control sexual desire and obsession. This is a very different frequency than the love that originates in the heart! The effects of entrainment are just as predictable as in the previous example: the music and the musician's intention (strong emotions put into vocals and lyrics, rhythmic patterns and repetitive phrasing) re-creates this state of animalistic mating need, even after it's natural benefit has passed, and it becomes a primary state of being. This is not sustainable. Without balance, it drives the artist and the audience alike into an unhealthy state within a relatively short amount of time.

This kind of imbalance is part of what I call *sound pollution*: simply too much of a natural thing. Now think about the Beatles for a moment, as another example. Their music has been celebrated for decades and is showing no signs of being forgotten. Their music displays a balanced repertoire, which I believe is why so many people love to listen to them. They have songs for every imaginable state of being: something for the rebel, for the reflective or religious soul, something for the rough rocker, wild party nights and something for light fun. It's all there. I'm certainly not claiming that the Beatles were completely balanced human beings – I'm sure the enormous pressure of world fame took its toll - though their ingenious balanced music may have saved them from losing themselves too much in the midst of their crazy ride on the wave of success.

You can go through the list of musical genres and determine for yourself which element of your soul each one expresses.

Connecting back to our theme of music for spiritual growth, we might ask ourselves what kind of music could align us with the highest aspect of ourselves, what kind of music conveys the frequencies of pure spirit and of our highest ideals, and what emotional frequency do we need to align to, in order to create such music?

There is no one answer to these questions, because I am convinced that it varies from person to person. But I do think that we will have to take Goldmann's aspect of *intention of the musician* into account when we search for the music that aligns us with spirit.

Music - since music is proportioned vibrations and everything is in vibration - is everywhere! The whole Universe is a glorious array of harmonic and discordant proportions. We humans are entirely created around the principles of music. So too, all levels of spiritual existence vibrate, "sound" in a certain way and we, as cosmic musicians, (and here I mean all of humanity; every human being) can be channels for any one of those levels. We have an important choice to make: Which state of being will we align ourselves with at any given time, in our way of living our lives, in our artistic expression and our musical entertainment selections?

In a way, I sometimes think that if I ever accomplish the vast ideal of understanding the phenomenon of Music fully, I will at the same time be holding the key to understanding the Universe. I am in no position to claim to understand music completely. But in struggling to learn its physical, psychological, mathematical and esoteric nature, I am working my way closer to understanding the human being.

Chapter Three

The Three Realms of Being:
Pathway of Manifestation

This following chapter looks closer at the philosophical aspects through the outline of basic esoteric content. While this discourse may seem irrelevant or difficult to access for some, please know that in the end, without exploring these elements of our more subtle realms of existence, our understanding of music, the human voice and human nature must remain incomplete.

I think most musicians will agree with me when I say: the music is there, even without us there to hear it. It is there as an *archetype*, the 'being of tones'. It exists as an eternal world of frequencies, geometry and mathematical principles, as the principles of harmonious and discordant relationships between all spiritual beings visible and invisible, and as the expression of those beings' ultimate purpose, their goals, their essential plans. I will call this the **archetypal realm**. This realm is universal; it is the same for everyone. It is like the toolbox for the composer: all the tones, scales, chords, rhythms and numbers are there as the universal law. The artists need to tap into those laws to choose the most fitting elements to help them express what they experience in their own soul.

There, in the individual soul life of the artists, the composition will begin to take shape as an idea, where it would already be audible to those who could read the artists' minds. Then the artists' task is to transform the composition that lives within them into an external piece: to make the idea audible for physical ears, as accurately as possible.

We must remind ourselves again that the principles of resonance and entrainment will always be a factor for our personal expression as well. Depending on the degree of influence we allow from other people and circumstances on our inner and outer life, we as artists express more or less of our own music (our own purpose), or more or less of someone else's.

A good piece of music emerges out of silence and ends with silence; it contains silence too: we call this silence within the music the *rests*. Several great composers claim that the rests are particularly important. Why is that, you might ask? Silence is to music like white canvas is to a delicate painting. Silence is not simply nothing. It is the place in which potential sound manifests before it becomes audible. It is here where we can anticipate future sounds or remember past sounds, where we imagine it, feel it and focus our inner listening on it. Think about it this way: How can I sing a song correctly, unless I hear it in my imagination first? And how is it that I sometimes already know what my friend is about to say, word for word? It is as if I "hear" it manifest between us first. In the same way, the *idea* of a composition or of an interpretation already manifests before it becomes audible. It "hovers" in the silence before the first tone, in the imagination of the musicians, the lifted baton of the director about to begin a great symphony, in the expectant listening of the audience. Even a simple exercise well done comes into being that way. I would like to call this realm of manifested music in the *inaudible stage* the **potential realm**.

This realm is much more personal, more individual to each artist, than the *archetypal realm*. Here, we can "hear" our tones and compositions before we play or sing them. Some singers speak of "*audiating*" a tone in their minds before singing it. Reaching into this *potential realm*, we use our focused listening and our engaged will forces (action) to manifest it into the **audible realm.**

To Summarize:

1 The Archetypal Realm (The Realm of the Spirit)
This is the realm of Mathematics, Geometry, Proportions and Harmonics. From here, these universal principles can be manifested into the Realm of the Soul for different aspects of artistic expression:
Architecture, Mathematics, Geometry, Music, Colors, Language, Sculpture...

2 The Potential Realm (The Realm of the Soul)
In this state, the medium of expression and manifestation of specific aspects out of the *Archetypal Realm* has been chosen. This could be any creative process, visual or performing art, writing, design, cooking, children getting ready to play... The form of the creation is hovering in the realm of ideas, feelings and mental pictures of the creator. Also, from here the experience of art imprints itself onto our soul and our bodies' energetic patterns after the creative process is completed.

3 The Audible Realm (The Realm of the Body)
This realm is specific to music and the spoken word. (For visual art forms this realm would be called the *Visible Realm)*. Here, through the engagement of our will, the sound is made audible out of the *Potential Realm* and is now felt and heard through the physical senses.

The music will continue to exist in the *potential realm* of each listener and musician after the last tone has ceased to be audible. It does not simply disappear. As it goes back from the *Audible* to the *Potential Realm*, it imprints itself on our physical being, on our souls, into our memory. It is not the same as it was before it became audible. It will be quite different for different people, even if they heard the exact same piece of music: it now has been shaped and colored first through the performer's unique personality, his/her emotions and mental pictures that came up during the process; it has then been received by the audience and has been again shaped through each listener's mental pictures and feelings as well. In addition, the audience's intent, their active tuning into the *potential realm* significantly contributes to the sound quality and overall performance of the artists. Each artist and each listener now carries a unique memory of this music in their personal *potential realm*, colored and individualized by the process of its performance and its reception.

Without the element of silence we brush over these delicate transitions. We fail to give the music its own space! More and more musical productions in our time entirely eliminate the silence. And yet, in that silence lies the chance for focusing one's attention, for initiating active listening into a higher realm, for touching the other musician and our listeners in spirit, in joyful recognition. In short, eliminating the silence skips the part in which the inner soul movements and transformation, which are initiated through the music, are anchored into permanence. Without rests there is not enough time to digest and process. Indeed, eliminating the element of silence hinders the development of some of the essential human capacities which music can help us achieve: the validation and recognition of the other beings and the harmonious, fine-tuned cooperation and connection between us and the cosmic whole.

In our modern, western culture we are struggling with the imbalance of too much physical sound and not enough time and space to process it within the active silence of the *potential realm*. Just as there is also too much waste, too much clutter, too much food, too many images, there is also too much sound! The problem is widespread and severe and, I'm sure, it comes as no surprise to anyone. The question is so important, I would like to ask it once again:

*

How do I meet such a cluttered world?

How do I add my voice to it without getting lost in the cacophony?

*

Chapter Four

All the Parts of our Miraculous Vocal Instrument

*

What makes our voice work?
How can we learn to control our voice?
How does it get its unique sound?

*

Anyone who embarks on the fascinating journey of vocal development will soon realize that their practice requires attention to, and mastery of, a whole lot more than just the throat and larynx. They will realize that the elements used to shape and cultivate their voice include every aspect of their being: physical, emotional, mental and spiritual. Each one of these aspects has a direct influence not only on the sound of our voice, but also on all the other elements of this complex instrument. Understanding how this interconnected system works may allow us to approach difficult or unconscious aspects from alternative angles. This principle has been taught for centuries through different yoga practices and martial arts: connecting consciously to the more subconscious worlds of feelings and mind through the mastery of the physical body.

   Here are some examples of these complex interconnections. We could create a much longer list, but here is a start:

Aspect of our Being	Has an Immediate Impact on:
Thoughts Feelings	Breathing pattern Tone placement
Listening capacity Sound processing	Speech formation Focus Rhythm
Intention Focus	Listening capacity Imagination Breathing patterns
Posture Enunciation (speech sounds)	Breathing Capacity Attitude, Feelings Sound color

Aspects of our Being are Working Together to Create our Unique Voice

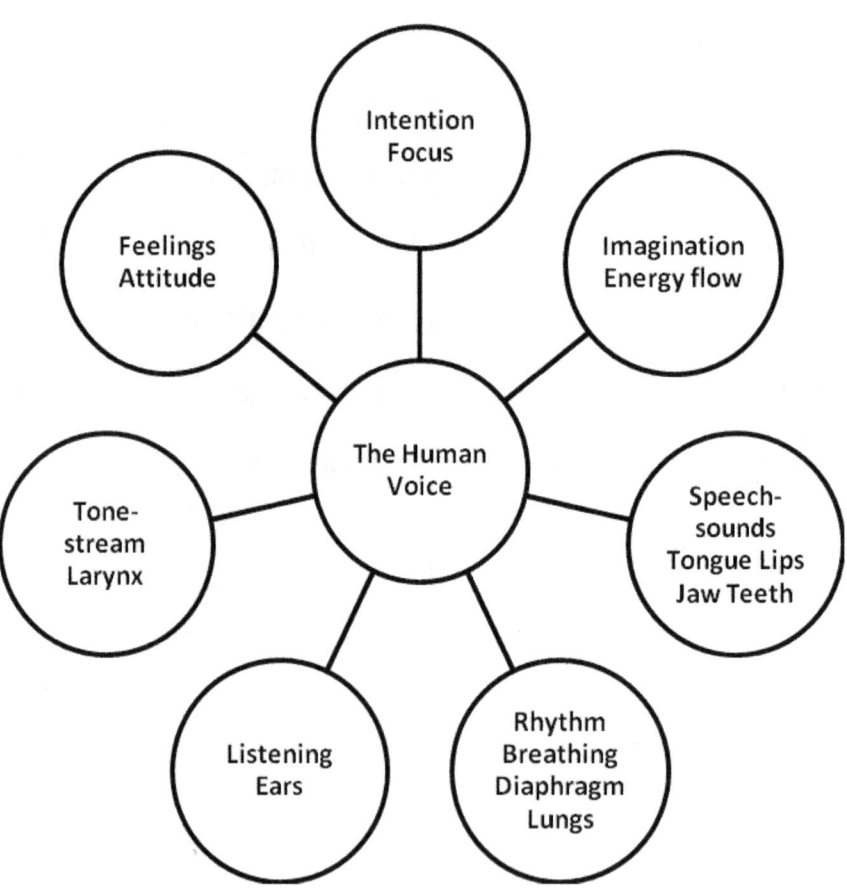

The following thoughts about these essential elements of our singing instrument are not meant to be a scientific examination and explanation of each aspect, nor a technical instruction manual. Rather, I am sharing my experience of each element's role in the activity of singing and how it plays into our journey of inner development. These different parts of our instrument are always interconnected, and in reality it is not possible to separate their activities in our vocal training; however, for the sake of clarity I have made an attempt to separate them here in this chapter.

I do strongly recommend studying the physiological side of our voice as well, although we will not take time for this research here. Comparing the symmetry, forms, repetitions and variations in the structure of our bodies has something very musical to it. You may choose to study, for example, the shape of the system of ears and larynx as they appear in a certain relationship to each other. That same shape-principle can be found again in the systems of kidneys and bladder, ovaries and uterus, lungs and heart. What do these systems have in common? To ponder the divine wisdom of the body can teach us so much! But for that you will need another book.

Posture and spatial awareness

Every musical instrument needs to be held and handled in a very specific way to create the desired sound. This is no different in the case of our voice, where the instrument is our whole body, head to toe. We could even include the room we are singing in as part of the instrument. Our body-posture therefore needs close attention, in order to provide an optimal physical vehicle for our voice.

It begins in the feet: How do I maintain the contact with the floor? Let it the weight be distributed evenly but with enough flexibility to shift it in all directions. Then the knees: are they flexible or are they locked? Keep them unlocked as if balancing on a gently rocking boat, and about hip-width apart. And as you move upwards through the legs, ask yourself: are my hips aligned and my lower back comfortably balanced and straight? Is my solar plexus area open? Align and lengthen your spine to allow plenty of space for your diaphragm to move. Is my heart space open? Where are my shoulders in relation to my chest and back? Make sure your shoulders are not pulled up towards your ears or slumped forward, causing your heart to retreat. How am I holding my head above my spine? Does my chin jut forward or up or does it droop? Keep your neck flexible and as long as it can be and imagine your whole face as the elevated light of a light house, shining down slightly below the horizon.

There is a lot to consider, and some more severe misalignments cannot be corrected in a singing lesson alone. The best help for possible problems with posture comes from therapeutic movement- and structure specialists, though a singing training can offer fairly comprehensive general instruction.

Misalignments in the posture often highlight ailments or emotional blocks that in turn can cause a number of difficulties for the singing voice. Look around you: there might be someone whose shoulders and upper back are slumped, their head and neck collapsed, their heart-space retreated. Such a person might look like he/she is afraid to show their true size and power and choose instead to appear submissive and slightly depressed. Through this posture the breathing process is compromised right in the middle, in the area of the solar plexus – like a kink in the garden hose compromises the flow of water, with this obstruction the diaphragm cannot move at full capacity and in turn our breathing becomes shallow and inefficient.

Or have you seen someone whose shoulders appear to be pulled up and fused with their neck, looking square and tight? I experience such a person as wearing thick armor over a tender and vulnerable inside. The focus of energetic patterns is pulled up around the chest, and the belly area is a bit neglected. Often such people have an audible tension in their laughter, that illustrates their inability to be truly relaxed and joyful, or they laugh too much and too loudly and it seems to me that their forced merriment serves as a cover for the well hidden pain inside.

Often I see people craning their necks in an effort to "reach" the high notes they are trying to sing. This shift in the posture puts pressure on the throat and creates precisely what the person is so diligently trying to avoid: the high notes are out of reach and the voice sounds pinched and strained.

I also frequently work with students whose knees are tightly locked while standing, causing their hip-joints to lock in response and the whole lower body is under lock-down. As a result, the breathing cannot reach the full instrument as it stays caught up in the upper chest region; this is the area where the breathing patterns of stress, fear, insecurity and grief are centered!

Sometimes I see those who seem to "drop" all their energies down into the lower body and have a slackness and lack of energy around their upper body. Their vibration is too slow! This is the archetypical slouchy teenage-boy posture that sometimes stays on as a tendency into adulthood. Here, the control of the pitch and volume is often compromised and the person struggles with controlling their communications and endeavors – be it singing or anything else. An inner tiredness as part of the personality is apparent. It is almost as if the digestive system has taken over. In fact, I sometimes wonder if this is indeed a problem of the metabolism and can be changed through a rigorous shift in exercise and dietary habits.

Have you seen people who catch your eye, even clear across a public airport hall, because their walk is tall and upright, yet flexible and alert? Or you can't help but admire someone who is gracefully holding their head high but not their nose? Or maybe you have seen someone who, as you could tell just by looking at them, was kind, intelligent, attentive and humorous? Have you ever seen a tiny person who outshines their surroundings because of how they carry themselves? Those are often the ones with the best sound in their voices.

When I teach larger groups of people, I often begin by asking them about their experience (or lack thereof) with singing. Even some of the ones who tell me they have never sung in their lives, might immediately catch my eye as potentially fabulous singers: I see the inherently beautiful voice through their excellent posture and attentiveness, through their warm expressive speaking voice, their joyful way of communicating and their souls' allowing for new connections. I am always right: these people do not "learn" to sing; they simply discover that they can.

As we spread our awareness further, beyond our body's boundaries, and notice how we are in relation to the room we are in, we can begin to include our surroundings in our singing. We can allow the spatial planes above and below, front and back, left and right to become part of our sound space. In my experience, becoming spatially aware of my environment requires *listening* even more than looking.

Ears and listening

I am often asked how I managed to almost completely lose my German accent in just a few years? Well, I'm sure it is in part simply a knack for language, but I believe it is the ability to hear details in the sound formation and to reproduce what was heard. The ears are working together very closely with the larynx and the whole set of muscles in and around the mouth like a well coordinated team: the ears (or the mind, when the point of reference comes from a sound memory) give the commands, the larynx and mouth respond. The more differentiated and trained the listening (and consequently the musical memory) is, the better trained and awake the responding organs are, the more precisely we can create the sounds we want. Just like an untrained visual artist might know exactly what a cat looks like, but to be able to actually draw a cat accurately, the artist's hands, mind and eyes must be well practiced and trained!

It is very important to realize that the organ of the inner ear is also responsible for spatial orientation and balance, which are in turn absolutely essential for accurate sound processing. In addition, having two ears provides us with the experience of "stereo reception". Having two points of reference allows us to locate a sound's source with relative accuracy, and to have awareness of our body's positioning within our environment. People who have lost their hearing in one ear have told me that it took them quite a while to develop a new way of orienting themselves in space.

We know that in order to develop a certain level of musicianship, to attain an understanding for melody and harmony and particularly to be able to sing in tune, our hearing needs to be in good working order; now we also know that a healthy inner ear is responsible for balance and spatial orientation. Our musicianship and ability to sing and our sense of movement are very closely interconnected! Therefore, mastering space-coordinated, rhythmical movements like dancing, and/or Eurythmy is in my opinion an essential skill for a well rounded musical education.

There are indeed elements of spatial awareness – awareness of geometry, ratios and proportions - in the way we process, understand and create music. So many times when I help an inexperienced student learn how to hold a tune, it turns out to be simply a matter of helping him/her aurally find a spatial framework for the musical intervals and scales. Several beginners have gone with me from appearing to be tone deaf to holding a melody correctly within a short amount of time. Those quickly progressing beginners had already developed their instruments' foundations by becoming good listeners, keen observers and graceful movers with a clear sense of their surroundings. These are well focused, imaginative people eager to try something new. All they needed was someone to show them how to use their instrument and how to cultivate it.

The need for a good orientation in space and time extends into the soul-life of the singer. I have had some students who may even have claimed to be able to sing fairly well but then, in our initial conversation preceding their first lesson, I noticed that they were not able to feel comfortable in their own space. Some are reluctant to fill it and attempt to become "invisible." Some had trouble quieting their own minds while listening to my words, thus cluttering their mental space; some were not sensitive to setting time-limits to their own speaking and more often than not had trouble honoring my physical private space and time. Those people have much more difficulty making progress in their singing work. For such students it is important to understand that their listening skills, their mastery of movement, spatial orientation and rhythm may need to be established first, before a healthy singing voice can be developed. Such singing lessons then require a very different format in order to meet these needs.

I would like to add here that bone conduction (our bones resonating with the sound of our own voice as well as external sounds) also plays a central role in accurate hearing. If we pay attention to the vibrations shifting within our body, we can develop a keen whole-body sense for nuance that the ears alone cannot provide. I once heard someone tell of a young deaf woman (whose inner ear was intact) who learned to sing, simply by feeling the vibrational shifts she created with her voice. I do believe that to some extent this is possible.

Breathing and diaphragm: our rhythmic system

We have been breathing ever since the moment of our birth, day and night, reliably sustaining our oxygen flow throughout the body, never having to pay any special attention to the activity of breathing. Of course, we all learned this in school: our breathing serves to replenish the levels of oxygen to our blood. But there is a lot more than just that to be said about the purpose of this *central rhythmic* element! First, air is also the vehicle for sound. There is no sound in a vacuum! Second, our breathing is the bridge between inside and outside, the means of exchange between our inner world and the world around us. Thus, the breath is the vehicle of sound which carries the content of our inner world to the outside. If we want to deliver sound consciously and precisely in order to express eloquently or musically our thoughts, feelings and reactions to experiences, we must learn how to control the vehicle!

Our breathing changes with the different modes of being, just as the heart rate does. You can explore this yourself and watch: how does a sleeping person breathe, versus one who is driving a car? How do you breathe when you are happy? How does anger influence your breathing pattern? What happens when you laugh? When you cry? When you create a piece of art or when you play sports?

Realizing the importance of the breath for the energetic modes of our body, numerous ancient and modern methods of meditation and prayer as well as martial arts have paid close attention to the breath and its application, in order to develop physical strength, focus of the mind and emotional self-control.

Our largest voluntary muscle, the *diaphragm*, is dedicated to facilitating the expansion and contraction of the lungs. It also keeps the heart in a gentle, rocking motion, as the heart sits right on top of it, between the lungs. The diaphragm has the wonderful capacity to work closely in sync with the *abdominal muscles*, to allow very precise control of airflow. Mastering the interplay of these muscles in a healthy way allows us to develop incredible subtleties in our singing voices, but also to take charge of our emotional field and our overall well-being. In fact, not only do we respond to our emotional state with certain breathing patterns, but we can also in turn influence our emotional state by choosing the breathing pattern we prefer. What an incredible power this mastery can give us over our emotional state of being!

Although anatomically of course incorrect, it is easy to imagine two air chambers: one in the belly, one in the chest. We use the chest-air for yawning, deep sighs or for running hard, but we also tend to favor this high "air-chamber" more when we are anxious, stressed or afraid; our chest heaves with sobs when we cry; the belly "chamber" on the other hand moves more when we are relaxed and content, but also when we are focused on creating something, when we are listening, when we are amused; we feel these muscles after a good belly-laugh. Good martial arts teach us that our power center lies in the belly, rather than in the limbs. Bringing the breath into this lower "air-camber" in the belly and developing flexible yet strong, conscious guidance of our breathing rhythm helps us bring balance into our feeling life and it is of course essential for a healthy singing voice. The rhythm in music as well as in our lives in general is the element that provides order and structure in all aspects of being. It provides the framework we can rely on, it is the essential aspect for connecting to other musicians – or to our environment in general.

What happens when the rhythmic system is out of balance? Just picture this: A lady following the fashion of her time in the 18th or 19th century was wearing a corset; her abdomen was so tightly restricted, that the only way to breathe was shallow, and high in the chest. Such ladies were known to be emotionally fragile, anxious and to faint easily. Once the ladies began to protest the restricting corsets and began wearing clothing that allowed for more freedom, someone who preferred the image of the anxious damsel-in-distress came up with very posture-altering high heels! If you've ever tried to walk, run or even just stand in those, you'd have noticed that in order to keep your balance, you'd have to shift your alignment in such a way that the center of your breathing has to be up high in your chest again... which relates to the breathing patterns of insecurity, distress and anxiety.

Often in my singing courses I have students who come with fears, judgments, worries and other imbalances. Just focusing on the balanced and more conscious guidance of the breath in the activity of our singing exercises has lifted many participants out of stress, anger, frustration or depression.

V. Werbeck Swärdström warns us that every time we make progress in our vocal development, the breathing needs to be re-learned and re-established: as the voice grows, the vehicle must adjust as well. She also points out that regular practice is needed to keep the breathing in our awareness: more than 3 days without practice, and we will need to put our rhythmic system in order again.

Rhythm is so much more than the tick of a clock or even the

steady beat of a heart. There is rhythm in the tides, in the seasons, in day and night. There is rhythm in the way we walk, the way we speak, the way we grow; in the way we perform our daily tasks. Rhythm has to do with *time*. There are fast rhythms and slow ones, complicated rhythmic patterns and simple ones. Every planetary system has its rhythms; there is rhythm in the way we take turns in balanced conversations, there is rhythm in the way we alternate work with rest. If there is imbalance in the rhythm, things will fall apart sooner or later.

In the world of music an imbalance of rhythm has immediate and quite obvious chaotic consequences, while in our every-day life we often forget this law of rhythmical balance and imbalance. We might stay idle too long, or work without resting until something has to happen to provide enough shock for a wake-up call! Every mode of being evokes a corresponding rhythm: our heart-rhythm quickens when we get excited and slows when we relax; our breath is slow when we are slow; we breathe faster when we walk faster; we pant when we run. Our ability - or disability- to align our sense of rhythm to the rhythm of our surroundings and our momentary situation is even manifest in our vocabulary:

Do you remember the expression that someone is "off-beat?" or "tact-less?" Or "in/out of sync?"

Rhythm will determine the character of a piece of music even more than the melody or the harmonic arrangement: it will set the mood for an up-beat song or a slow one, it determines whether one can dance to the music and what the dance might look like. Rhythm is the primary factor that allows us to create music together and move together as a group, by providing a reliable framework in *time* that all participants can agree to. To move and create sound together in a rhythmic fashion is incredibly empowering: it builds up our life forces and at the same time organizes and coordinates our mental awareness. There is a wealth of very rhythmical and repetitive work-songs in all traditions of folk music, with the single purpose of sustaining, empowering and synchronizing the work of the singers.

Thus, learning to have a good sense of rhythm extends our musicianship into our everyday life.

Larynx and tone stream

Although we could, from a strictly physiological perspective, agree that the vocal chords (located horizontally in the center of the larynx) and the intricate muscles suspending and surrounding the organ are the primary source of the human voice, I find that they are merely a point of transformation. Here in the larynx, sound input is received and transformed into an active response. Even when we do not make a sound, our larynx measurably responds with tiny echo-like movement to every sound we hear. Children regularly adopt their parent's speech patterns, inflections, habits and their choice of voice coloring so closely, that it is easy to hear the resemblance between a young adult's voice and their parents'.

This emulation can be observed in adults as well. Have you noticed that when you attend a lecture where the speaker uses his voice in a pinched, strained manner, your throat begins to get sore just from listening? And many people in the audience begin to clear their throats or cough. Or, on the other hand, when you have the privilege to hear a live concert of a singer who understands the art of effortless singing, you walk away feeling thoroughly warmed up and ready to sing yourself?

Not only external sounds move our larynx, but our inner triggers do as well: our feelings, our energy and mental pictures passing through us can be transformed into an audible, energetic vibration; every word, every sentence we utter is colored by the feelings and underlying intentions! We make feelings audible through our larynx even without language, for instance by laughing out loud at a good joke or crying with strong emotion. And we make thoughts and mental images audible in many ways, for instance by singing a song that was stuck in our head, or by speaking our thoughts out loud. In short, much like a telephone-receiver that "translates" electric signals into sound, our larynx receives energetic vibrations from the *potential realm* and transforms them into sounds for the *audible realm*. In the larynx vibrations, thoughts, feelings and mental images are received and translated into sound. It is a place of manifestation, a place of transformation, a place of communication.

Tiny bones and an astounding number of muscles and cartilage are intricately moving together to create the tones we intend to speak or sing. Just like any musical instrument is not able to produce any music without the musician, the larynx alone would not be able to create the sound we experience in a human voice. For our voice to become audible and recognizable the whole instrument, which includes our whole body and energetic system, is needed to shape, amplify and color each unique voice. Our body, with its high percentage of fluids, its air-filled spaces, more or less toned muscle and hard bone structure is highly receptive to vibrations, and thus is capable of amplifying, supporting or hindering the sounding of the voice. As each body is unique, each instrument sounds unique.

Although each voice's basic sound capacity and general range are determined to some degree by genetics and development during the formative years of childhood, we can still significantly influence the color, quality, flexibility and strength of our voices by training, shaping and moving the throat-muscles and energies around our larynx, mouth and respiratory system.

The human voice is shaped not only by the unique structure and proportion of each individual body, but also by our environment since, as I mentioned before, the larynx - and in fact the whole speech/sound/breath system - reacts with tiny movements to every sound we hear, like a faint, echoing imitation: a potential for a response.

If we consider the larynx' and throat's characteristic of reacting to all sound in the environment, we come to understand why many voices in our time sound pressed, crowded, sometimes even damaged by the constant overload of sound input! The most obvious remedy here is the cultivation of silence: to offer this delicate instrument time of rest and replenishment. Here we can clearly see the intimate connection of the larynx to the ears and the reality that these two organs are indeed so strongly linked that it is difficult to separate them for explanatory purposes.

The question of what difference there might be between 'tone' and 'sound', if any, comes up frequently among my students and with good reason, since these two words are often treated as synonyms. In my understanding, the noun "sound" can be either a musical tone, or a broader spectrum of vibrations, including sounds (noises) like water, traffic and musical harmonies, while "tone" is specific to music, referring to a specific pitch. We usually choose the word "sound" (either as a noun or verb) when we speak of the quality and the coloring of a voice.

Those who have studied and are working with the "*School of Uncovering the Voice*" recognize, in addition to the precise proportions of scales, harmonies and intervals, a streaming characteristic in the melodic sound element as well as in the speech element. We simple call them *sound-(or tone-) stream* and *speech-stream*. Much more fluid than the idea of individual words or individual tones, these two modes of sound manifestation are experienced as a connecting flow between the 3 realms of manifestation. These two streams are frequently entangled and, to the untrained singer, appear to be the same. But as we develop the singing with our exercises, we soon discover that in a free singing voice these two streams appear separated, working closely together without disturbing one another. Good singers are able to maintain a free, cohesive sound quality throughout their songs while still being able to enunciate every word accurately, while untrained singers experience a kind of competition between the two at first: either the words are clear and the tones sound pinched and disconnected, or the tones are well sung but the words cannot be understood. As we practice our exercises, we aim to separate these two elements in our awareness, so that the *speech stream* colors and shapes, but never interrupts or compromises the *sound stream*. Both of these streams are flowing out of the *potential realm* into the *audible*, directed by our intention and imagination.

Speech sounds and tongue, jaw, lips and teeth

The approach to speech-sounds in the *School of Uncovering the Voice* is quite unique in that, while we are establishing our posture, breath, movement and space, we begin guiding the tone of our voice primarily through consonants: M, N, V, R, L, Z, NG etc. This is a surprisingly new concept for many, but is usually embraced and recognized quickly as a safe-haven, within which the heart can remain unexposed while the ears and the mind lead the sound-stream into new pathways, lifting it out of the confinement of the throat and filling the head and the space around the head, the "cupola," with tone. In doing this we are learning to utilize sound space for our instrument. Soon, the beginning student discovers that while they may allow for more volume, vowels tend to be emotionally exposing and seem to have a mind of their own; they tend to make us light-headed, self-critical and tempt us to strain the voice. Consonants on the other hand allow us to focus and remain objective.

Vowels, like tones and melody in the music, belong to the realm of soul, dreams and feelings, while consonants, like rhythm, musical structure and harmonic proportion, are the elements of consciousness. You know how very tired or intoxicated people tend to slur their words? Their consciousness is so compromised that the consonants, the elements of consciousness, are disappearing! On the other hand, you may know someone with a high level of alertness and intelligence who has no trouble enunciating their words, but may struggle with relaxation or melodic expressiveness in their voice. When we are truly balanced we use vowels and consonants equally, we are in balance between dream-state and consciousness, we move rhythmically between sleeping and waking.

When we sing, the melody and sound element (vowels) are much stronger than when we speak – consequently, in order to make sure the lyrics of our songs are still intelligible, we must pay particular attention to the accurate enunciation of the consonants, in order to maintain the balance.

The complex muscles in and around our mouth are constantly shaping and re-shaping the sound-space of our instrument as we speak, creating the subtle overtones and colorings unique to our languages and dialects. The more we learn to master these muscles, especially the tongue's muscles, the more accurately we can create the specific sounds we are aiming for. Exercises for the tongue and lips relating to each other and to the teeth through consonants and tricky sound-combinations, vowel sequences and consonant-vowel transitions are designed to facilitate that mastery.

In fact, this mastery is so important in this approach to vocal development that we cannot afford to lose part of our attention in the meaning of sung words. Beautiful exercises with "nonsense" syllables and sound combinations instead of words allow students to focus completely on the shaping of the speech - elements and the guidance of our sound.

The *Jaw* is the only bone with movable joints in our Skull. (There are tiny movable bones in our middle ear, but we have no control over their movement). It is like the limb of the head, where all the movement and action is happening. We open and close our mouth many times a day and yet, when it comes to singing, most of us need constant reminders to open up and relax. Why is that suddenly difficult? Opening the jaw is experienced by so many as a relinquishing of control, a breaking-down of the barriers we have so carefully built up to protect our weaknesses; or we may associate a slack jaw with diminished consciousness and low energy; we might feel that a relaxed jaw is in conflict with the happy facial expression we want to maintain for our singing; we might be worried that if we open up, others might hear us and we may not want to be heard. They might judge us and notice that we don't sound so great – so we tighten the jaw and keep the sound trapped inside. The result is that we indeed don't sound so great. A vicious cycle! A relaxed jaw does in reality not constitute diminished consciousness or loss of control, but rather provides us with the necessary flexibility for accurate movement and shaping of sounds. As we learn to relax the jaw, we actually gain better consciousness and control over the shape and color of our sound than with a tight jaw. Once we have mastered the jaw we can project our sound effortlessly, even with closed lips.

As we can see, much of our progress in vocal development has to do with our willingness to adjust our mental images, beliefs, judgments and expectations. Once we know what to listen for, what we want to hear, what to visualize and how to imagine our sound and energy streams, our voice will follow.

Imagination and energy flow

One day we were sitting at our dinner table, having a lively conversation about the various events of our day. My daughter, who was then about eight years old, was listening intently, as I was recalling my new little group of beginners: adult students in the Waldorf Teacher Training who had never sung before and did not know how to carry a tune at all. My task was to remedy that lack. My daughter became very quiet and looked thoughtful. Then she spoke up:
"Mama? If these people never sing and don't even know how - what do they have in their heads all day long?"
Good question! Our family members are all so used to having songs in our heads, accompanying (and sometimes annoying) us throughout the day, coloring our minds, sometimes becoming manifest in a little humming or whistling, or in full song!
"Oh, I'm sure there are pictures, sounds and words in their heads" I answered her.
"I know, Mama, I know - but they need songs in there, too."
my eight-year-old was very clear about that.

What do we have in our heads all the time? Sometimes there is no room for our own songs: music is offered in every store now, in every car radio, I-pod, TV-set.... but everything is fed to us from the outside, none of it our own creation. Singing along helps a little - and many people do sing along to music. But turning the electronics off and singing our "own" songs (or writing our own stories or poetry, painting our own pictures) suddenly returns to us the power to decide and control what we have going on in our own heads!

Once we decided to actually sing and explore our own vocal capacity, questions might come up:

Eva Cranstoun

*

Where is the primary impulse for my singing activity coming from?
Where do the commands for moving from one tone to another originate?

*

My teaching is full of vivid imagery, because in the imagination we can create and cultivate living, moving pictures which create moods and feelings that will shape our melodies, add color to our sound quality and smooth out our phrasing, correct our pitch etc.
It is important what kind of image we choose – the wrong ones will influence our sound just as much as the right ones:

We may see dry pebbles in a row or step-ladders while we sing - and our songs will sound choppy and bumpy; or we can imagine flowing water or smooth train-tracks or raising fog - and our voices will flow smoothly through the songs.

We can imagine reaching up for the high notes and having to stretch and labor to get there - and our voices will sound strained and thin; or we can imagine creating space for the tones to fit into the instrument and experience the sound streaming on a horizontal plain.

We can reach and search for the tones from below and risk compromising our pitch; or we can aim at them from above, touching them lightly or firmly, like a xylophone.

We can imagine our energy-stream reaching down into the ground as we sing an upward movement, and we can imagine effervescent levity, to float our voices while we sing a downward movement, balancing our voice's tendency to be subject to gravity and consequently 'flat'.

We can imagine growing roots and simultaneously being suspended like a marionette.

We can imagine resting our center on our kangaroo-tail, spreading our cobra-hoods or unfolding our angel-wings.

We can imagine sitting in a pool of water and with our arms creating currents around us...

The images are many. As we begin to hold these imaginative pictures of energetic movement in our minds, we will gradually develop a clear sense for the actual flow of energy through and around our body while we sing. This is much more effective than trying to control our organs and muscles directly.

Vocal development and the improvement of sound quality, as we approach it in the *School of Uncovering the Voice,* is done to a large extent through the imagination and through growing awareness of the energies flowing through and around us. Letting the mind wander instead of using directive mental images while singing will compromise the voice greatly: mistakes happen, harmonies are lost. Thus, healthy singing-practice schools us to become masters of attention through claiming control of the content of our mind. This work can then ultimately become an invaluable element of spiritual development.

The *School of Uncovering the Voice* has recognized this strong esoteric component and has been consciously developed with the intent to stabilize the singer's physical and mental health and to cultivate integrity and spiritual awareness.

Following Werbeck's intention, throughout our vocal studies we should work with questions like the following:

*

What kind of sound - and tone quality would best support our physical, emotional, mental and spiritual well-being?

*

I suggest that this ideal tone-quality we are listening for could be described as objective but also warm, gentle yet powerful, alive, universal, archetypal; it must be flexible, effortless, and consciously changeable, depending on what and where we sing and whom we sing for; we must explore the boundaries, the "edges" of our vocal possibilities in volume as well as range without compromising the gentle flexibility.

We have already found that our posture, our feelings and our state of consciousness significantly influence the sound of our voices. But there is another element that we are cultivating in this approach that brings about the *healing and regenerating* aspect of holistic singing: the *life-forces* or so called *etheric forces*. This is the kind of energy that causes living cells to re-generate and grow.

If you ever participate in a course of the *School of Uncovering The Voice,* you will likely hear the expression: "*the etheric tone*" used among more experienced students. What is meant by that?

It simply means that the well-sung tone is filled with life-forces, that the sound-stream is laced with, supported and buoyed by these regenerative, etheric, effervescent energies or *levity-forces*. In contrast, the *gravity-forces*, which we all are subject to, are the forces which, if they are given too much power in singing, can cause the voice to sound pressed, off-key, heavy, inflexible or narrow. In the cultivation of the effortless tone, the restricting gravity forces are balanced by the expansive levity-forces we also call "etheric". When we figure out how to do this, suddenly the sound-stream comes alive with flexibility, effortless accuracy and richness in color! Allowing our singing voices to sound with these regenerative energies, we can experience a healing process not only in our own well-being, but also in the listener's. Singers who work with this aspect experience that their voices seem to stay "young" and flexible much longer; listeners feel more alert, energetic and balanced after hearing such singing. Actual healing can take place.

Please note that the listener benefits from this phenomenon ONLY in a live situation, not through a recording, since etheric forces are not recordable.

How do we accomplish this? We can cultivate awareness of levity and develop more and more the ability to infuse our tone with life-forces by guiding our energy, imagining it with our mind, but also through dynamic rhythmical work. Rhythm generates etheric forces.

How does such an esoteric approach to singing work with the feeling life? Here, too, we strive for mastery of our feelings, in order to have the freedom of choice in interpretation and overall well-being:

Feelings and attitude

The popular, modern idea that music and singing are primarily a means to express our personal feelings and to make our personal affairs known to the world, has caused millions to renounce any attempts of song, for fear of exposing themselves and of being judged harshly and unfairly. This practice of publicly exhibiting our private issues through songs has caused many popular voices to become over-loaded and distorted with emotion. Please do not misunderstand: there is nothing wrong with songs being sung with deep feelings, and we do often need such an outlet for our profound or turbulent emotions. Music is called the language of the soul for good reason! The mistake we have made here is simply that we tend to forget how music and singing in particular has so much more to offer than just being a personal emotional outlet. Many have forgotten the connection, forged through music, between spiritual content and individual soul content and have become limited to the soul content only. To think that any kind of singing would always lay open our most private, personal being and require intense emotional involvement is detrimental to our society, because most of us prefer to protect our privacy: we have given the activity of emotional song over to professionals who are willing to expose themselves and entertain us, while the rest of us have become mute and passive.

Millions are now missing out on their uniquely human capacity to sing, to join in common sound with others, to create music and companionship, to clear their minds, connect to their spiritual essence and enliven their hearts through their voices.

Singing can become an expression of a higher level of our being, because it is also a language of the spiritual world, a means to communicate between the spiritual world and the world of soul, a means for spiritual content to reach into the depth of our being without needing words. I think this is the reason why we imagine angels to be singing: they are the messengers between us and the spiritual world. When we are searching for a voice-quality to help us find this connection to our spiritual aspect again, we must strive for the kind of sound that manifests something more universal, clearer, in addition to what my own clumsy emotions can offer. This objective voice - the "Angelic" voice - will be able to facilitate raising my own being into a higher mode of existence.

  Our state of being, our emotions color our voices. Everyone has experienced a friend's voice on the phone. Even though we cannot see our friend physically, we can still tell what kind of emotion is living in the other person, because we can hear the laughter in his or her voice; or the tears; we can hear anger or boredom, fear or defensiveness, enthusiasm or concern. It is all there, audible, because it colors the voice as it travels through the vocal instrument. The different emotional vibrations change our breathing pattern, our heart rate, the tension or relaxation in our muscles, the workings of our metabolism, our ability to think. Many people, when asked about what music and singing has meant to them, reply that it has to do with their feelings. Songs they listen to create associations with their feelings; songs they sing or hear help them express their feelings. Much of the music we enjoy is exactly that: an expression of feelings, often very personal. The music we listen to awakens and enhances feelings in ourselves, and the music we play and sing evokes feelings in our listeners. There is great power in that! We can express, trigger, enhance and grow fear, desire, anger and egotistic motives in others, or we can use this power to plant and cultivate hope, clarity, inner balance, humor, joy, love and interest in others. In other words: it depends on the intention of the musician.

What if you could find a state of being in your feeling life, create a reliable "backdrop" for the singing that is universal, objective and safe, yet personal at the same time? Would you be willing to sing?

*

Consciously harnessing the power that our feelings have over the sound of our voice, is an important aspect of an esoteric vocal development. We need to take charge and decide what our singing will carry into our own organism as well as into our audience's. We must cultivate a positive attitude as our point of departure. More than that, we must find joy:

No matter what I sing or whom I sing for, I begin with joy as my backdrop for my art. I choose to imprint loving joy into my own organism and my audience's, every time I sing.

This unattached, loving joy seems more of a state of being, an attitude if you will, rather than a feeling - it can transcend immense sadness, frustration, anger or lethargy for anyone who can find a way to access it at will. In my experience, this backdrop of joy is adding a kind of warmth and universal familiarity to my voice that touches my audience very deeply, no matter what I sing. It also helps me to lift myself above my own, personal concoction of feelings. In this way I can sing, even though others around me are crying.

Many people are afraid to sing because they are afraid of being judged. Most likely there had been a bad experience in their life that caused them to believe that their voice is worthless. Sometimes this past event was not so much experienced as an attack on their singing voice, but on their value as a person in

general. Such harsh judgment is sometimes entirely unintended, but it frequently hurts the receiver for many decades.
I hear this story repeated, in many slight variations:

- *" When I was in fourth grade, my teacher told me to just mouth the words and not sing"*

- *"When I was ten, my brother told me to stop singing, because he said it sounded ugly"*

- *"When I was eight, I sang in a children's choir and the girl next to me said that I sounded like a duck"*

- *"When I was a little boy, I loved to sing. I sang a lot. One time I was interrupted by my father, who said I sounded terrible and it was time I stopped behaving like a girl "*

- *"In my family I was always told I could not sing and that I should not waste my time getting on other people's nerves with it"*

... This list goes on.

Do you realize the power some people from our past hold over us? Do you realize that we tend to allow those who have passed harsh, often unfair and untrue judgment against us, to have powerful influence on how we view ourselves, while those who have encouraged us and validated us seem to have comparatively little impact on our self-perception? Our lives would indeed enfold very differently, if we chose to allow positive validations and encouragements to determine how we view ourselves, rather than the demeaning negativity of a few. This is an enormous lesson to learn for almost all of us.

Too often do I have to gently convince the little girl or boy inside a 45 year-old, that their music teacher in 4th grade was wrong; that the teacher simply did not know how to show them what to do, and instead accused them of having no voice.

Finding, connecting to and embracing one's long-lost singing voice frequently becomes a sacred act of forgiveness, healing and tremendous inner growth.

Intention and focus

In Chapter Three we have explored the idea of music living as an ocean of lawfulness in the archetypal realm, being guided and shaped by our creative minds in the potential realm, and then flowing into the audible realm as tones, like a river and re-joining the music in the potential realm of our memory as soon as we release our tones into silence. Imagine that we as singers and musicians are simply joining into this already existing stream of sounding energy, by allowing it to flow through us, by giving it space and a vehicle, rather than being the source of it. How much less effort would you need for singing, if it simply meant learning how to allow space for the already present music, rather than having to produce something completely new out of your own being!

If you are willing examine this thought a little more, you may experience an essential "change of mind" with this perspective. A new imagination of our energetic involvement begins to dominate our singing: if the music and all the parts of our vocal instrument are indeed already there, rather than having to build a brand new instrument and create a new sound, we can simply learn how to remove the obstacles in our already existing instrument and invite the already existing sound to stream through us. We merely need to learn how to guide it and provide the best possible space for it. We are offering myself as a servant to the music:

We are inviting the music to express itself through us, rather than using the music to express our individual personality.

Do you see how the direction of the intention is reversed? Not only does this perspective eliminate the danger of an exhibitionistic attitude, it also permits us to validate and express the spiritual aspect of music. On the journey to develop the singing voice, we begin with this perspective as our starting point. But it will also become a destination, a goal for our vocal development: when we truly find this objective state of being in our advanced singing work, it seems as if the sound sings through us without us having to add any personal effort. All that is needed then is our intensified listening and attention, allowing and creating space for the music to manifest. Everything else will ideally have become physical habit and will not require our awareness. This is the aspect of our vocal development that V. Werbeck-Svärdström calls "Reflection of the Sound."

Chapter Five

What Healthy Singing Can Teach Us

When practicing exercises alone or one-on-one with a teacher

Every day of our life, waking and sleeping, we have been breathing. Most of our breaths are unconscious, always in motion, keeping us alive without requiring a single thought from us. Our breathing is always there, responding automatically to our every mood and action, every emotion and state of mind. But we can take charge of this life-giving marvel of breathing, stopping it at will for a time, speeding it up, slowing it, deepening it, changing its ratio at will.

In the *School of Uncovering the Voice* our singing exercises always begin with the balancing and organizing of the breath, by bringing it into alignment with our movement, sound, mental focus and listening. Practicing these "first exercises" is like readying a room before an important event. It helps us put our being into "real-time" – if we have been stressed and running on adrenaline and little sleep, these exercises will finally show us our body's primary need for rest: we will get sleepy. If, on the other hand, we have been idle and sluggish, lazy and slow and sleeping plenty, these exercises will help us connect to our unused store of energy and we will feel awake and ready for action.

Moving forward from there, other exercises will then provide opportunities to shape and control our muscles in and around our throat and mouth, our tongue, cheeks, lips etc., penetrating them with consciousness, while listening and observing intently. We have been using our vocal instrument all our lives, we learned to speak our mother tongue without troubles, we "know" how to

string syllables together with ease, we have the inflections, pauses and subtleties of speech ingrained in our being – and yet, when we isolate and re-arrange these speech-elements, strip them of meaning and examine them, separated from our everyday use of language, we might suddenly realize how little awareness we have of our sound and speech instrument.
Here is a small sample of the many challenges we must tackle:

*

Where and how exactly is this "NG" sound formed?

How do I smoothly connect an "NG" sound with an "A" sound?

How do I roll my "R" and how does my breathing play into it?

What is a pure vowel vs. a diphthong?

How do I choose the coloring of my tones between bright, warm and dark?

Why is it that we suddenly struggle to relax our jaw?

*

We may notice with surprise that it is difficult to pay attention to all the parts of the singing-instrument at once. We are getting to know our body, maybe for the first time intimately, consciously.
   Practicing alone or one-on-one with an experienced teacher will bring us face-to-face with our shortcomings and our own harsh judgment against ourselves. Setting *realistic* goals and working towards them each practice session or lesson is essential.
For example:

" Today I want to focus on relaxing my jaw and my forehead."

Or:
" Today I would like to work on intonation in descending phrases."
"Today I will work on equalizing my tone color between the different vowels."

You get the idea.
  It is secondary whether we actually reach the set goals perfectly, as long as we mindfully and objectively work towards them. Gradually, we must find a 'YES' as an honest answer to each of the following questions:

*

Was my goal realistic today?

Can I forgive my imperfection and continue moving towards improvement without faltering?

Can I be joyful yet objective, observe myself and be my own teacher?

Can I sustain mental focus?

*

Listening to my own exploration and practice with loving and forgiving attention, yet at the same time with objective and scientific scrutiny, teaches me to take on the ancient challenge the Greeks gave those entering the temple of Apollo in Delphi:

"Human Being, Know Thyself!"

When singing in a choir or large community

With "choir" I mean a large group of people, say 15, 20 or more. We usually associate the term *choir* with an organized group, divided into 'sections', usually with a leader/director who is studying, rehearsing and performing choral music.

In addition to the traditional choirs there are many ways communities share songs, be it on the ball-park, in churches, for birthdays or whatever other gathering we can imagine, where people who may not even know each other suddenly, maybe spontaneously, align to some extent with everyone else through song. More often than not, these songs are not sung but shouted, out of tune and lacking harmony. But even through this common mode of shouts and silliness there is a way for everyone to connect for a moment through these songs. Imagine the impact they could have, if these opportunities of musical connection also held the benefits of wholesome singing! In musicians' circles, common birthday songs often take on a new dimension through harmonizing feats. There is hope yet for those little abused ditties!

Connecting with a group of people through sound and rhythm, through breathing and imagination can teach us to develop awareness of the others around us and how to add our own valuable contribution, without disrupting or dominating the whole group or getting lost in it.

I remember at school (I went to a Waldorf School in Vienna, Austria) we would recite poetry together as a class. I can still appreciate how difficult that was, to unite thirty unique ways of speaking into one stream of speech through breathing together, finding and agreeing on the inflections of the voice, aligning our imagination, agreeing on how long to pause, where to speak softer or louder, when to slow down - how musical it was! All elements of music were there, except the tones and harmonies: listening, rhythm, breathing, tempo, pauses, focus, imagination....I loved these often quite long poems in the upper grades and high school, contemporary poetry, ballads and elegies and excerpts of dramas and epics. Since we were able to unite in that way, singing together in tune and with intricate harmony was only one small step away, and we mastered that beautifully as well.

Once a good choir can create such refined soul-connection among its members, once the group is able to find a sound-coloring that is like one whole new being and not just the sum and jumble of individual voices, the audience is invited to join into this connection at every performance. A strong bond is formed between those who listen in silence and those who listen while sounding. Audiences can find it easy to experience the music deeply, and tears of joy among listeners are often part of such performances: everyone, performers as well as audience, are in that moment touching on a profound truth of humanity, the truth that we all share a common spirit, we are connected on our deepest level of being. Listening, moving, sounding, breathing together, allowing ourselves to share the same vibrations, will give us a glimpse of this Oneness.

When singing in a small ensemble

By *small ensemble* I mean a group no bigger that maybe eight to ten people, or even as small as a duet. The smaller a group of singers is, the more responsibility lies with each individual to provide the correct notes, rhythms, harmonies and dynamics to the songs. For each singer to be able to hold his or her own part against the harmonies of the others, a fairly high level of musicianship is required.

Ensemble work is in my experience really about consciously establishing a balance between our sympathetic and antipathetic tendencies.

Generally, the vocal learning process generally swings from an initially sympathetic mode to a primarily antipathetic mode, until finally the student will master a balance between the two. When beginners learn to listen more intently than normal, they automatically move into a primarily *sympathetic* mode at first, and thus tend to get "pulled across the table" to join the other voices, rather than staying in their own part. They need to allow for a little antipathy to join into the mix, differentiating their voices from their fellow singers'. They need to develop just a little more auditory self-awareness. Once they begin to be more reliably conscious of their own tone placement within their body, they can guide their own singing in harmonic context to the other parts, rather than moving their voices in unison with them. Eventually, the harmonies the other voices add become helpful *points of reference,* instead of a distraction.

If the small ensemble is a group of *beginners*, this learning sequence explains why singing harmony is usually not possible until everyone has developed enough awareness and mastery of their voices. Only then can they confidently hold their part accurately, standing next to someone who is singing something else entirely. In my small group voice-lessons we usually begin this process with 2-part rounds or simple short exercises and scales sung in 2 parts. The progress of each student's musical abilities in this setting, however difficult the initial challenge may be, is much faster for each individual than in a larger group.

In order to resist the sympathetic tendencies, many students are tempted to fall into a kind of *competition* against the other members of the group. The group becomes louder and louder, as the singers attempt to be stronger than the other parts, afraid that they would otherwise get lost and lose their focus.

Instructing the group to *sing very softly* while practicing singing harmony works wonders for improving intonation, rhythmic accuracy and confidence. It is a most significant step towards transforming our inner attitude of competition. Thus, singing together can become a vital stepping stone to moving out of competition into cooperation in freedom.

You don't need to be louder than your neighbor, because if you are, you will lose the awareness of the other singer and your harmonic point of reference for your intonation will be gone. Allow the others' voices to be equal to yours. Allow your voice to blend into the harmony and know that every voice counts! This is what healthy ensemble singing teaches us so accurately: how to work together as a team.

> *This is what we as humanity must learn now, if we want to survive the current crisis on this planet: to listen to, validate, support everyone else, while responsively and accurately fulfilling our own task; to recognize that our part is no more or less important than our neighbors'; to admit freely and lovingly that our survival is no more essential than our fellow humans' on the other side of this little planet; to learn to live with one another and in awareness of each other, with the attitude of established ensemble singers who have mastered their art – then we will be able to adapt and move on to a new level of consciousness.*

For a small ensemble of more *established singers*, the challenge of having to overcome the now more prevalent *antipathetic* forces stays persistent for quite some time: we are facing the challenge of coordinating highly individual 'soloists' to create a blended sound, where no one is more or less important than another, without losing his or her unique sound quality.

When an advanced ensemble works and rehearses in cooperation rather than with an appointed director, this task of *finding equality* does not only apply to the voices, but is reflected in the group's approach to communication:

*

Can we work together without a leader?
Do we interrupt one another, or do we let each other speak and value each end everyone's contribution? Are we showing true interest in each other, are we appreciating each other's genuine effort and commitment to music?

*

The constant human need to receive validation for our professional abilities and our contribution is an enormous driving force for many musicians, although often entirely subconscious. To make matters worse, the world of music in our time is so highly competitive, that the very survival of a professional musician is dependent on his/her competitive attitude. And yet, in order to be able to sing harmony and become a proficient ensemble singer, we must give up our competitive approach and be willing to cooperate with others. Isn't it astounding to realize that this art form of singing, which in its holistic form can offer humanity almost everything it needs for its advancement of consciousness, is so strongly dominated in our time by a the very same force that it must teach us to transform. I will repeat: we must learn to move from competition into cooperation in freedom. Our life depends on it!

I have seen an interesting phenomenon connected to this issue appear in some groups of professionals: although they are, as professionals, capable of excellent teamwork, blending and exquisite dynamics in the field of music, they choose not to use these same skills on the level of social interaction: competition, jealousy, conflicting opinions and power-struggles as well as debilitating self-doubt and criticism abound. Their music may be technically excellent, but frequently lacks the warmth and magic a different attitude would convey. The intention behind the music, the attitude of the artist strongly influences their musical performance! It is one of my biggest hopes that such gifted professionals would realize how simple it could be to transfer their musical skills to their social skills, by extending their musical studies to the realm of holistic and esoteric connections. They would find that such new-found awareness and depth will in turn add a new and exciting, positive dimension to their art that they had never been able to access before.

When singing solo in public:

Why, we should ask ourselves, do we want to sing solo, or why not? What is it that appeals to the artist and what is it that appeals to the audience, when we sing solo?
The safest way for me to approach this question is to share with you my own experience.

1) It's a gift that must be shared: although it has always made me terribly nervous, I have always wanted to sing for people even as a child, because I have always been able to touch people's core being: I love seeing them open their hearts, seeing the listeners' frowns melt into relaxed smiles, seeing eyes glistening with joyful tears; I love feeling the same gratifying warmth and joy I experience when giving a gift to a friend, that turns out to be exactly the right thing.

2) I need truthful validation: of course, I like being validated and complimented for what I have given. We all do, don't we! It confirms not only our work, but our very existence and our value as evolving spiritual beings. Applause is addictive. But did you know, that a surprising number of performing artists are not easily content with their own performance? We are our harshest critics! Sometimes it is surprisingly difficult to accept praise, because we are never quite sure if it is spoken in truth, or in well-meaning ignorance. I like to call it *validation* or *appreciation* instead of *praise*: it sounds more truthful to me. In our culture (especially here in California) praise comes often too quickly and without much thought to the value of the performance: "good job," we say. What does that really mean? We often just like to make others feel good and we shy away from truthful feedback. Because of that, I take my primary cues for the much needed feedback, appreciation and validation from facial expressions and body language first, and from those I can hopefully interpret the words correctly. But even more importantly, once I had learned to forgive my own shortcomings and imperfections and validate myself the way I would like others to do, the true recognition from my audience suddenly began flooding in.

3) I facilitate an expression of soul and spirit: When I sing solo, I am a stand-in for the aspect of *aloneness* of the human being, with all its challenges and blessings. I carry the full responsibility, but I also have the full freedom of interpretation. I willingly expose myself to the scrutinizing judgment from others and from myself, but also to the deeply grateful appreciation of others and of myself. Thus I can choose to stay alone and separate, or I can decide to delve deeply into connecting with my surroundings through my performance. In other words, I can, as a soloist, decide out of freedom to connect with my fellow musicians and my audience. Through this soul-connection, I take on the role of an ambassador between two aspects of the human being: the *Oneness* and the *Separateness*.

I become a representative for all those listeners, who can benefit from this image of a lone singer: I am demonstrating that I can take on my task, I can own my contribution, I can align myself with my accompaniment (if there is any) and I manifest something of value out of the spiritual realm that can touch, comfort, uplift and transform others and myself.

4) I can impress my mode of being upon my listeners: on one hand, popular artists are connecting people across otherwise impossible differences. Many thousands of people, for example, are enthusiastic followers of one particular musician, but they don't know each other. Yet they are connected profoundly through the music of this one artist, whose mode of being influences all his/her listeners' lives. What a responsibility, what a gift, especially if the artist's mode of being is wholesome, balanced and inspirational! On the other hand, this same gift also carries a potential problem, because if this artist's mode of being is imbalanced and troubled, if it is angry, depressed or obsessed, then through *entrainment,* this artist impresses his troubled being onto thousands, who feel understood and enjoy listening to music that expresses their own troubled inner lives – and thousands more, who feel troubled and imbalanced *because* they are listening to this particular artist's music, because the artist's mode of being has "rubbed off" on them. But if I am able, as a solo singer, to connect my being to the spiritual reality of the Universe and become a conduit for it, if in this way my voice can carry a state of timeless presence, joy, compassion and love from that divine source into the world, then an immense stream of healing sound will be passed on to my listeners through my voice. It is my deepest wish to be such a performer:

*

Not "My Will" but "Thy Will be Done"

*

When singing solo in private:

You may think singing in the shower, in the car or while cleaning your kitchen does not count. Think again! If you are on your own and you sing, whom do you touch? Who is listening, who is performing? Who is doing the expressing, the transforming? It's all you! It is Baron Münchhausen, the legendary German General all over again, pulling himself out of the muck by his own hair and saving his own life in one of his tall stories.

There have been days in my past, when my body was too tired to perform the simplest tasks; or days when I was so scared and disheartened, that I felt I could not speak a word. There have been days when I felt so cornered by the enormous impossibilities of life's challenges, that I had no music left in my mind. But I still went to work, I still went to my lessons, I pulled myself forward, overriding the temptation to give up. And unfailingly, every time singing entered the scene, whether it was because one of my own children asked for a song, or because it was time to teach or take a lesson, my mood lifted, hope returned, smiles became possible, my mind cleared.

I still encounter days like that every now and then – but now I know the cure: I begin humming a simple tone sequence or a complete melody, or I fill the house with my full sound capacity. Sometimes I am amazed at the force of my body's resistance to singing my way out of depression or frustration, how much willpower it takes to sing in spite of it all! But I sing – and it lifts my soul.

It is as if the singing replaces the heaviness of my mood with a different state of being. The substance of music is lighter, more organized and lawful than the emotional medley of doubt, fear, frustration, overwhelm etc. When I sing, I raise my vibration out of the victim mode to a level of wakefulness, that allows me to take back the control over my inner and outer life.

True, at times when I sing my way out of my pain, tears flow, but I anticipate that now: it's the only way. The pain of my emotional turmoil is very real; it occupies my space like debris. When I bring in my voice and my songs, awakening myself and cleansing out the debris, pain will be dislodged, will rise up and leave my inner being, breaking through the surface of my awareness and causing the cleansing tears to flow: it's nice to get it out.

Chapter Six

Evolving Humanity Through Developing Musicianship

As she recalls in chapter nine (conclusion) of her book, Rudolf Steiner once said to W. Werbeck Svärdström :
"If people would sing - more, and especially more correctly, there would be fewer crimes on earth"
  What a bold statement! We must pay attention, however, to his elaboration "...more correctly" – in which he clearly suggests that there is a correct and an incorrect way of singing. This may sound harsh and judgmental; who dares to tell an artist about a right or wrong way of expressing him/herself? We could probably understand this statement much better, if we replace the word "correctly" with the expression "in a healthy way" - which must be what Steiner meant.
  I have pondered this statement through many years of work with the human voice. Observing the subtle changes in myself, my students and colleagues, which this "singing in a healthy way" triggered in us, I have concluded that a wholesome approach to singing, with all its aspects of physical, energetic, emotional, social and spiritual awareness, provides very practical guidelines and tools for our general approach to life.
  I do not mean to rob anyone of their own joyous experience of discovery. The best answers do not arrive in books! They come to us from inside, through our own observation and practice, as we are continuously striving towards perfection and true understanding.
  So instead, I would like to simply offer you a few more images, elements of this connection between singing and how to be truly

human, in the hope that you will find your own, profound questions. Maybe some of my "food for thought" images will trigger your own answers.

Being active, finding balance

No one can sing or speak for you with your voice, only with their own; No one can refine your voice for you, only you can. No one can exercise your voice for you but yourself.

Do not get me wrong, it is very important to play music and sing for others, just as it is important to sing or speak for others if needed. In fact, I think it is most essential for our well being as humanity to have as much of this music and voice-giving a possible. But the effect of actively singing with our own, true and unencumbered voice is very different from the effect someone else's voice has on us as mere listeners. True, listening to a wholesome voice may be just as profoundly healing, but on a different level. Active involvement and striving for the refinement of our voice is indispensable for true, inner growth: We must learn how to express our truth, add our sound to the world. Singing certainly lends itself to this task.

We have developed into a very passive society. Too many of us are seemingly content with "having no voice". Too many of us would have so much music to share with this world, but have no relationship to their own sound; they have not been shown how to use the one, incredible musical instrument they were born with, their God-given, miraculous, most amazing musical instrument! They have become used to being silent; they don't know anymore how to raise their singing voices in praise, lament or pure jubilation. And yet, all of us still have a very fundamental instinct that tells us: we need music to survive. And as a result of this instinctual knowing, millions of us are passively consuming electronic music, being vaguely aware of its power to touch, whether to heal or damage, our very core-being. We are continuously under the influence of music, without ever truly understanding the nature of this permanent companion. Many of us are exceedingly uncomfortable in silence, without the constant illusory company of the TV, radio, computer or MP3 player.

*

When have you last walked into a store that did not play music to accompany your shopping experience? How many of us are bold enough to be comfortable while being truly in silence, alone with ourselves?

*

We have become too estranged from ourselves, seeking entertainment in excess and thus covering up our insecurities. But along with covering the insecurities and pain, this excess of entertainment also covers up our own capacities and potential for self-expression and creativity. We have come to be out of balance.

All the aspects of our being, spiritual, mental, emotional and physical need to be developed simultaneously, so we can continue our inner growth and to prevent stagnation. This equal development of all levels of being is what a wholesome education should provide (Waldorf education strives for that), and we must continue to strive for a continuation of this development as adults.

If only all mathematicians, scientists and business professionals would engage in artistic activities, while all artists would learn to do their math, help run a business efficiently or study a scientific subject! (Many artists do, by necessity, hold a job in one of these fields, in order to support themselves). Such wholesome balance is an indispensable prerequisite for us to become fully conscious as human beings. We need to achieve balance, in order to rise to a new level of awareness as humanity: balance between sound and silence, between rational and intuitive thinking, between socializing and solitude, between activity and rest... We might need to look towards the unknown territories of our mind and soul, in order to find the right aspect that will help us create this balance: In order to feel fulfilled as a human being we do need to develop mastery in more skills than just those needed to complete our paid jobs. How many of us can lovingly admit complete ignorance in one particular subject (for example plumbing, dog-training, knitting, tango, bread baking, playing the piano or drawing, to name a random list of skills) and then commit themselves to studying it with enthusiasm, without letting frustration and self-doubt cut the adventure short? Small children learn everything in such a committed way. They anticipate errors naturally and simply continue their efforts until they gradually begin to master their task. Adults are well advised to realize that they do still learn best that way, although they are often too impatient and judge themselves to harshly, when the natural mistakes happen.

As we realize that the ability to sing is sadly lacking in our society, considering its incredible benefits it should be at the very top of everybody's list of new skills to be learned. Learning to sing usually does not happen overnight. It will require patience, dedication and perseverance, like any other skill.

If we look at the structure of a good composition in the classical style, a symphony, opera, concerto or sonata for example, all the elements of this balance are there: you can find not just one, but several themes with variations; there are times when the music guides us to go inward, into a reflective mood, and times when the music leads us to outgoing, active, energetic modes; there are rests, soft and loud parts; there are places where it slows down or speeds up; there are moments of tension and discord that are resolved into harmony... the celebrated master pieces are perfect non-verbal images of balance. On an acoustic level, vibrating the message all the way into our cells, such music can teach us how to master our lives.

We don't need to be able to learn all the instruments of an orchestra to enjoy a symphony, and we do not need to become a solo singer to enjoy opera or any other vocal performance. But the full scope of appreciation for the masters will only be experienced if an effort is made to study music in some form: joining a choir, learning an instrument, taking voice lessons... It is time to take charge of our own vocal instrument, our own mind, our own creativity. We all must lovingly dare to face our shortcomings, appreciating the ever so spacious room for improvement and, without competitive jealousy, cultivate gratitude to the true masters in the field for providing their guidance and for sharing their gifts with the world.

On an even more individual level, the theme of passivity versus active involvement comes up again in our specific approach to singing. An inner shift into a higher vibration, a higher state of alertness must be made in order to move from mere speaking mode to singing mode. We can call this shift "engaging the will." There is a profound difference that can be felt quite physically between thinking about singing or wishing to sing, and actually singing. Initiative is required. In the case of singing, we must become inwardly even more active than we are when speaking - a difference in energetic involvement akin to the difference between walking and dancing.

Singing vs. speaking.
secrets of sustainable youthfulness

In modern vocal development we speak commonly about *chest voice* and *head voice* to distinguish two very different sound qualities in the human voice. Generally, the chest voice is more at home in our lower registers, while the head voice dominates in the higher notes. I would like to replace these two terms here with "speaking voice" (chest voice) and "singing voice" (head voice). This is another way of differentiating between the tone stream and speech stream discussed in chapter four.

It is possible to sing with the "speaking voice". Such singing has roughly the same range as our speech patterns and has a tendency to sound either metallic and harsh or breathy and sometimes a bit thin. Some people who naturally have a warm, sonorous speaking voice, can also produce a warmer sound when singing with their speaking voice. With some extra pressure applied, we may be able to add a few notes to our speaking-range on the top or bottom, but will soon find a kind of "ceiling" or "floor" that prevents us from finding the higher or lower register. In order to go to those registers at the periphery of our speaking range, we have to release the pressure and create more space for the "singing voice" to take over. Artists like Sarah McLaughlin have made this switch between the two voices into one of their trademark sounds.

When we speak with the singing voice, it sounds a little odd – as if we are speaking through a slight yawn, the sound sitting higher up in the head. With some careful training, it is possible to blend the two voice-modes together into a more unified whole – relaxing and opening the speaking voice more into the head space, and in turn using the chest as additional sound space for the singing voice.

In my work I have found that those singers who excessively use their speaking voice for 'singing' and apply pressure to achieve volume, tremolo and range, are the ones whose voices get prematurely tired and even damaged. Just recently a very popular singer, Adele, experienced severe damage of her vocal chords and required surgery to restore her voice. It remains to be seen whether she will fully recover. Listening to her low singing voice I can hear a lot of pressure that undoubtedly creates constant strain to her instrument. My guess is that if she does not change her technique (which she probably won't because it has become her signature sound) she will run into more and more problems until her voice will be damaged beyond repair. Many vocal artists today are facing this very physical dilemma.

The popular vocal techniques could be comparable with the modern culture of many professional sports. The majority of these amazing Olympic competitors can only participate in their particular sport for a certain amount of years before their bodies will suffer a serious injury, a permanent damage to ligaments, or simply get too slow. In the same way, many popular modern vocalists will scream out their songs for a few years within their limited range – and over time will need more and more technology to cover up for their growing vocal troubles. I would be very curious to hear the unedited singing voice of some of them. I can imagine many of these voices would be all but unrecognizable to their fans in their natural form.

In contrast to the competitive Olympic sports, the wisdom of many traditions of Yoga and martial arts, which take the flow of life-energies into account, shows a very different and much more sustainable approach to accessing physical power, controlling movement and staying healthy and fit. In fact, many such martial arts, for example Tai Chi, have been known to have a rejuvenating effect on the body as well as the mind.

Similarly in the realm of singing, songs sung with primarily the speaking voice will cause strain, damage and early aging of the voice, while songs sung with a balanced, holistically cultivated singing voice and a carefully integrated chest register will energize, restore and rejuvenate the voice even into old age.

The art of listening

Do you remember the children's game "telephone," where a secret message is whispered from one person to the next around the circle, and then the final version is compared with the original? I remember playing this game a lot, always amazed at the incredible transformation a simple sentence can go through. The reason for the shift is two-fold:

First, the compromised ability to really listen and hear the message, and *second* the difficulty with the accurate enunciation of whispered words. In other words, the problem lies in the hearing as well as in the speaking.

I have re-designed this game for my teaching purposes, to be played at conferences, workshops and group lessons: in the simplest version of my *musical telephone game*, one short musical phrase (maybe consisting of three tones and a simple rhythmical pattern) is sung by the starting person and sent around the circle. Everyone can hear it. The next person in the circle is to imitate it as closely as possible. Let's say the second person sings a slight variation of the original, without intending to. The third person's task is not to try to restore the original, but rather to pay close attention to the variation and then pass on the new version as accurately as possible: the challenge is to pass on what you heard, not what you think it should be! We can always observe a gradual shifting – sometimes the changes are very subtle, but they are always there. The greater the number of experienced musicians I have in any given group, the less the travelling phrases will change: musicians have developed their hearing and memory for subtleties in sound.

Looking more closely at the first of the two challenges in the telephone game, whether whispered or sung, it comes down to the same question: can we patiently and attentively listen to the whole message, or do we stop listening after we assume that we know what is coming? Can we listen to the message to the end, without rushing to conclusions, passing judgments and making simultaneous decisions on how to proceed, once it is our turn? A fundamental dilemma of human communication is excellently illustrated by a simple children's game.

This ability to quiet the chatter of our own mind while listening, accurately processing and then relaying the meaning objectively without judgment is, in fact, a musical skill.

I have drawn great inspiration and practical advice for further understanding communication skills from the book "Nonviolent Communication, A Language of Life", by Marshall B. Rosenberg, Ph.D.

The art of practice and self-awareness

"I can't sing for the life of me" someone told me recently. I will call her June. To my inquiry as to why she was so convinced that she was unable to sing, she answered that she had tried but to no avail. But as I asked a few more questions, it became clear that she had not taken any lessons or advice from anyone, had not sung as a child and had only tried a couple of times. She worked with me daily for a week – and found that she did have a lovely singing voice. She developed new confidence and experienced immense joy in the process.

I am confronted with this erroneous kind of conviction quite frequently, even some children have it now: it seems as if they operate on the belief that *'if it does not work instantaneously, it never will'*. But what we tend to forget is, that having talent is not the end of the journey – it's just the beginning! It simply is a gift from the universe to be used wisely. Some people's talent is even hidden, buried under many layers of fear, judgment and faulty expectations; the best talent is wasted on someone who is not willing to work and practice. On the other hand, anyone interested in learning a skill can do so to some extent with the right instruction and enough practice, even if initially no special 'talent' is detected.

One week was certainly not enough for June to really develop her new-found voice. It was just enough time for us to prove her old belief wrong – and now the real work, the practice could begin.

Practicing a skill takes us on a journey of self-discovery. We will meet elements of ourselves that we may not be so familiar with. Maybe a perfectionist like June will find that she needs to learn to appreciate and validate her own process, without expecting perfect results: she may have held herself in contempt for too long; an endlessly patient person may suddenly experience impatience with himself and realize that impatience can have a certain driving energy in it that can be quite invigorating; an over-confident student may suddenly find that his confidence can become an obstacle to his progress, obscuring important subtleties, while the extra-careful student may realize that a certain amount of abandon and carelessness is sometimes necessary for a new breakthrough. It is as if we were finally making friends with ourselves, as if we finally decided to get to know a casual acquaintance, finding depth, detail and nuance in ourselves where we had never previously anticipated it.

Have you had those dreams where you suddenly find new rooms

in your old house? Maybe in your dream, you suddenly discover a whole new floor upstairs, with precious furniture and big windows; or you stumble into a dusty attic that could use some cleaning, which you never knew existed. Practice can be like that, especially if we acknowledge that musical practice (especially in singing, since the instrument is our own body) is indeed a very powerful form of inner work, of meditation. We need to knowingly allow the spirit back into the music and into our practice.

The art of observation and non-judgment

To observe without judging is a very difficult task indeed, especially if my object of observation is me, but also if I am required to observe my student. Go ahead and try once to analyze, describe objectively what you see or hear without any personal interpretation (which is already a judgment). Describing a voice's individual characteristics and even its weaknesses without subjective comment is a true art that can take many years to develop. Any good teacher will agree that such observation is invaluable.

I will demonstrate:

Someone comes into my studio for the first time to take lessons. Her goal is to become a soloist. If I listen to her voice moving through several exercises and I think to myself: "this person should not be a soloist. There is too much basic work to do"... then I have already passed a judgment.

But the pedagogical or therapeutic observer *must* be able to interpret phenomena, in order to truly understand the challenges and to be able to come up with ideas for solutions. Therefore the teacher must develop an approach that comes out of the impulse of love and true compassion, an approach that validates the pure, untainted spirit that lives in everyone. Then we can ask the question: what is needed in order to remove the obstacles that hinder this pure spirit to come through? What can I offer to this human being to help him or her access their potential more fully? Having found a firm inner mode of objective non-judgment and compassion as a teacher has been a key component of my students' successes: feeling safe, heard and understood in my presence, allows the students to treat themselves in the same way. Self-judgment fades away and true self-observation becomes possible; only then can the student make real inner progress.

Below are examples of some objective facts I have observed with students. These are not all observations of the same person, but rather a collection of typical cases. In italics, I added *judgments, assumptions* that might appear in our minds with each observation, which can be counterproductive for both the observer and the one being observed. If you are ever observing yourself or others, please notice these unbidden thoughts as such but try not to give them any value whatsoever.

Pure Observation	Possible Judgments and Assumptions
There is noticeable pressure applied to the voice, which limits the range on both ends significantly.	Pushy and tense personality. She thinks she is already good. I'll prove her wrong –
The sound of the voice is bright, a bit thin, narrow and breathy with an artificial tremolo.	Someone taught her the wrong way. I don't like this sound. I prefer darker and richer voices.
The breath is centered high, above the solar plexus and in the shoulders.	She is nervous, superficial and probably not very bright; she is an anxious type.
The Jaw is locked into a fairly narrow position.	Humor is missing here. This one is a control freak.
Intonation is somewhat out of control on descending intervals and phrases.	Lazy ears. This one does not care to put any energy into her work.
Eyes and facial muscles are not engaged.	His mind must be cluttered with all kinds of unrelated stuff. He is hiding.
She has not much control of her posture	She looks like an old lady with that bad posture.
He appears to have no awareness of his off-key singing.	Why can't he hear this? It sounds terrible. A lost case.
New instruction is not processed very well.	How many times must I explain this? It's so easy!

So you see, even for one single student I might end up with a long list of several themes that will need to be addressed in our lessons. In order to provide constructive instruction, I need to be able to begin solving the problems I have noticed, while simply continuing to observe: the answers to the underlying issues will reveal themselves gradually. For example, I will be looking for answers to objective questions like the following:

*

Why is it this way?

How can I help the process of uncovering his/her voice?

*

By using an objective format, I differentiate, analyze and name the difficulties the same way doctors or therapists arrives at a *diagnosis*. As the teacher, I need to now decide for myself which elements should be worked on first and create a plan for lessons in the near future. In the process of my continuous, diligent observation, my inner relationship to my student grows into one of deep compassion and empathy. The student can instinctively feel safe to explore and make all the necessary mistakes, feeling assured that, although I usually don't need to specifically speak about this to my students, they know: *I will not judge them.*

The art of focusing

When my whole being is concentrated on the activity of singing or active listening, when I am completely focused on the tones and on following, guiding my musical phrases with my inner ear, a powerful mental clarity sets in. When my mind is free of cluttering thoughts and concerns, my inner space is free to be completely filled with music, cleaning out old patterns, dissolving hurts and stuck feelings and aligning my energies with the cosmic laws of music: healing can take place. I am always awed by the fact that time seems to become less linear in this state of mind. It is as if music, though called a *time-art* since it is performed in time, nonetheless transports me as the singer so completely into the present that the experience of time is very different during such focused sessions. Three hours can fly by and feel like 30 minutes. At the end of such a session it takes some mental adjustment to return to 'real-time,' just like waking from a dream. The level of alertness, available energy and intuition is unrivaled in this state of focus. It can take several hours and some deliberate slowing meditation to dial my vibration down low enough to be able to sleep.

I have experienced this kind of focus during my teaching sessions as well: even if I am not singing the whole time, I can, if focused, reach a level of intuitive knowing, energetic involvement and timelessness that allows me to teach several long sessions in a row without tiring: I do my work as if singing it. Wouldn't it be great if we could allways do our work in this way?

Chapter Seven

How to Get Started –preliminary exercises

In this section I would like to share simple, preliminary exercises for you to explore. These are not meant to be a replacement for a teacher, but rather an encouragement to find one. Also, these are *not* original exercises given by Valborg Werbeck-Svärdström, but have been designed by me out of generally applicable universal elements of her schooling, to give my readers a glimpse of this work and some basic elements and tools they can use to begin cultivating their voices. If you are interested in learning more about the specific exercises given in the *School of Uncovering the Voice,* you will need to work directly with a certified teacher. At the end of this chapter I have made a few suggestions to help you choose a teacher.

Please realize that, unless you already have an excellent awareness of your body and sound, following these directions on your own you might make mistakes you may never notice. This is my disclaimer for exercises gone awry. Don't let that discourage you, but rather take it as a part of my instruction.
If you have a friend to do them with, the two of you can take turns observing each other. That's already much better than working without anyone. I have added points for you to observe. Working with a mirror is also fun and immensely helpful at times.

Finding posture (A)

- Sit comfortably and upright at the front edge of a chair, feet flat on the floor, hands resting relaxed on your thighs or hanging by your sides.

- Imagine being a marionette, suspended by a string attached to the top of your head, like an elongation of your spine.

- Now imagine the puppet player who is holding you lets go of the string – let your body sink into a slouched position with an audible "fff" out-breath (not forced!), your head still facing forward.

- Now the puppet player gradually pulls you upright again. Relax your jaw, belly and throat and observe the air gently re-filling you without effort.

- Back in your upright position, hum a tone in your middle range, not too low, gently. Any tone will be fine. Feel amused, and let the amusement show on your face!

- When the tone is done, have your puppet player let go of your string again and let your body sink into a slouch with an audible 'fff' again. Do not take a breath between the tone and the 'fff'

- Repeat three to five times.

Finding posture (B)

- Now as you hum your tone, imagine the puppet player moving other strings, coming off the side of your shoulders, that rock you very gently side to side; there are strings attached to the center of your chest and between your shoulder blades, that gently move you forward and backwards, and in all 4 directions until you move in a relaxed little circle around the vertical center axis.

- You can change directions and play with the size of your circle. Imagine the center of this circle to be the center of your chest, your heart-space. Let your body respond. Imagine the string holding you up from the crown of your head continues to support your uprightness.

- After a few rotations, gradually allow the movement to come to rest, aligned with your vertical center axis.

- Make sure you never hold your breath during this exercise!

- With another "ff" out-breath, let the puppeteer drop the string once more, collapsing your body into another slouch.

- Now pull yourself upright again. Imagine, each time you straighten up, your spine becoming long and flexible. Upright once again, you are ready for another hummed tone.

- Any tone will be fine, but try for a different one than the first time. If you are familiar with a major scale, you may choose the first 3 tones in your preferred scale: 1-2-3-2-1. Dance your little circle around your heart-space once again. Smile.

- Repeat three to five times. Never forget to hum softly in the suspended position and during the gentle movement, feeling amused, listening inside yourself.

Establishing spatial awareness (A)

In this exercise you will stand. Remove your chair so you have plenty of space all around you (3 feet in all directions is good).

- Your feet should be about shoulder-width apart and parallel. Jiggle you knees as if "walking" without lifting your feet: now your knees are unlocked.

- Feel your arches: clench your toes and stretch them out again, feeling the even distribution of pressure from your weight on your soles.

- Line up your arches vertically with your knees. Gently bend your knees lower and straighten them just enough to be relaxed and not locked, as if standing on a gently rocking boat without holding on.

- Line up your knees vertically with your hip bones: imagine little pendulum weights hanging off your hip-bones. You want them to be aligned with the knees, not in front or behind them.

- Tilt your pelvis forward and backward to explore where your hip-bones are in relation to your knees. It's like belly dancing!

- Now line up your hip-bones with your shoulders the same way. Circle your shoulders, pull them up and drop them again, pull them backwards and forwards and roll them in gentle circles to explore where your shoulders are in relation to your hips and knees and how they can be aligned and relaxed.

- Now line up your ears with your shoulders. Gently tilt your head sideways left and right to experience where your head is in relation to your shoulders.

- Gently hum a sustained tone, as you hold your awareness of your aligned body, focusing on the different parts in turn. Ad subtle movement to help you focus your attention. Hold the tone only as long as it is comfortable, but as long as you can. Then simply let your jaw go slack and allow air to flow into your body.

- Try two or three other tones.

Establishing spatial awareness (B)

Remain standing. Make sure you have space in front of you for bending down.

- Now stretch your arms out sideways, including your fingers, in the cross- shape. You are now in the position of Michelangelo's human figure within a 5-pointed star.

- With a *hummed tone*, gently round off and relax your body and your arms gradually, lowering yourself downwards until you are crouching, curled up as small as possible close to the floor, head relaxed between your knees, in a fetal position.

- Support your balance with your hands on the floor.

- For the last little bit of your curling-up, release your

voice and finish the movement with an "fff" out-breath, emptying your lungs WITHOUT pushing, just so you are comfortably empty. In you fetal position, *wait* for your body to tell you when it's time to get more air.

- When you feel the impulse to fill up, gently release your position and gradually un-curl like a growing fern: straighten your legs first (but don't lock the knees) while keeping arms, head and spine still relaxed.

- Straighten your spine one vertebrae at a time, starting at the small of your back. Resist the temptation to raise your head! Remember, your head is attached to the very top of your spine, so naturally it's the last part to straighten up. When you straighten your upper back, make sure your shoulders are aligned again.

- When you feel that you are as tall as can be, raise your arms again to point sideways. If you want, you can gently raise yourself onto your toes for a couple of seconds. While you straighten up let your breath flow naturally in and out. Avoid gasping for air or holding your breath!

- Repeat three times or more.

Aligning sound, movement, breath and imagination (A)

You will sit in your chair again, as in the first exercise.

- Imagine sitting in a nice warm hot-tub or a beautiful calm lake, the water surface at solar-plexus level.

- Now imagine using your arms and hands to create currents around you in the water. If you open your hands but keep the fingers fairly close together, your currents will be easier to direct. Now imagine how the water will flow around you if you bring both hands from the sides in two wide arches towards and all the way to your belly, completely immersed under the imaginary water's surface: a current is created that pushes your lower body backwards a little, your lower back is rounded off, while your upper body remains vertical. The surface of the water touches you now slightly higher up on your body.

- Now if you reverse this motion, water is pushed away from your body and pulls you forward a little: the lower back straightens out again, the surface is back at solar plexus level. Can you see it? Play with this imagination for a while. Move it.

- Try to find a rhythm in it: each direction gets approximately the same time span. Imagine moving like Kelp – there is never any moment where the movement halts or skips.

- Now use your voice as well: Hum one of your

friendly, amused tones as you bring your hands in towards you belly, then reverse the movement in silence.

- Move on to the next tone in the scale and hum again, as you bring the current in an arch towards your belly.

- Make sure you don't sing into the part that's meant to be silent.

Things to observe (though not all at once):

- Am I really reversing the movement accurately?

- Are the two directions approximately the same length? The tone can be a bit longer than the silence if you'd like, but make sure the direction of the movement is lined up with sound or silence. It is always good to let the tone go just a moment *before* you reach the turn-around point in your movement.

- Is my imaginary water-surface and the influence of the current still where it is supposed to be, or did the water rise up to my chest?

- Did my hands come out of the water? Put them back below the surface.

- Is it really silent in my outward-movement, or am I audibly gasping for air? Listen for the silence, listen for the next tone that is about to come in.

- Is my humming relaxed, or are my teeth clenched? Un-clench them.

- Is my throat straining, or soft, flexible and relaxed?

- Is my facial expression worried, bored, tense or relaxed and friendly? Smile a little.

- Are my hands coming in all the way to my belly, touching and arriving there, or is the movement incomplete? Finish it.

Aligning sound, movement, breath and imagination (B)

Do this exercise only after you have thoroughly familiarized yourself with exercise 1.
Stand upright.

- Check your posture, as in exercise 2.

- Make sure your belly is soft and your shoulders are lined up and relaxed.

- Rest one or both hands on your belly, thumb on the belly button.

- With some space between your teeth and above your tongue, hum a tone. Any tone is good, but choose one in your middle range, not on the very bottom or top. As you hum, your belly gently moves in, making you gradually thinner.
- When you feel that you will be out of air soon, let go of the tone BEFORE you run out completely! Finish the out-breath in silence.

- Simply relax your belly and simultaneously open your throat and jaw. Air will flow into your body without effort.

- Resist the temptation to audibly gasp for air and to breathe high into your chest. Instead, observe your belly filling out again and KNOW that you have enough air for another tone.

- Now while you hum you will mentally count, as if counting steps in a comfortable walking pace: 12 counts for your tone, 4 counts for the relaxation that lets in new air (In-breath).

- Choose the next tone up and repeat. Go 5 tones up the scale this way, then descend again:
  1-2-3-4-5-4-3-2-1

Things to observe:

- Am I letting go of my tone at the right moment?

- Am I taking full advantage of the time I have for the expanding and in-breath?

- Is my belly moving properly?

- Are my shoulders and chest relaxed and held still on the in-breath?

- Is my counting only in my mind, or is it audible as little impulses in my tone? Smooth out those little impulses until they are completely inaudible. Do your best to keep the counting in your mind only.

Running your "range-wheel"

For this exercise you can stand or sit, but standing is preferred.

- Yawn. While you yawn, smile and make a sound. Even better, say something while you yawn and smile! For example: "Ah! I'm glad to be here!" Or anything that helps you smile. If you don't know how to yawn on purpose, I suggest you explore this at a time when you are naturally inclined to yawn.

- Observe how your voice sounds and feels very different from your regular speaking voice. That is because during a yawn our throat opens very wide, to allow more oxygen to pass through to the lungs. This extra space is our body's natural attempt to offer more oxygen to the brain in order to stay awake. We can use our throat's ability to create extra space to provide more room for air to come OUT as well, and to provide more unencumbered space for the voice to move through. It's really quite simple: a bigger instrument will have a stronger, fuller sound than a smaller one, so let's not keep it smaller than it needs to be.

- Now prepare your throat and jaw as if you are about to yawn, but then don't – and instead freely, without any specific pitch as the beginning point, aim your voice fairly high – and let it descend in a beautifully arching sigh: AAAHHH! Now aim just a little higher: AAAHHH!

- Now include your arms and knees: generously reach your arms up and, aiming upwards in your mind, then bring them back down in a gesture like a gentle waterfall as your voice slides downwards through your range.

- Allow your knees to respond.

- Let the movement naturally swing itself out and start over.

- Do this at least three times.

- Imagine the voice coming from the inaudible high above your head, becoming audible in your vocal range and disappearing again below your feet. Imagine that your sound it is much longer and much wider in range than what is audible.

- Now start from the bottom and let your voice soar upwards, like a drawn-out question. There are no pitches or specific tones to worry about here. Just toss it up into the sky lightly and let it go whenever it flies out of sight.

- Adjust the arm-movement accordingly.

- If you like, you can also experiment with reversing the body-movement: moving the arms upwards as the voice descends, moving the arms downwards as the voice moves upward.

- Now let your "voice –wheel" run up and down smoothly, but instead of imagining an up-and-down motion, think circular, like a large ferries- wheel.

Things to observe:

- Is my arching sound covering every little spot in my range, or am I skipping over some parts of my range? Can I smooth it out?

- Is my body-movement properly lined up with my voice's movement?

- Am I opening my throat and jaw without pressure?

- When I allow air to flow into my body, is my belly expanding as explained in exercise 3?

- Is my throat space staying open for the in-breath, or collapsing? Keep it open!

- Am I joyful?

- Am I focused?

- Am I listening?

Finding inner stillness and joy.

For this exercise you may sit or stand.

- Think of a favorite song from your childhood, a hymn from church or maybe a little song you have sung to your children. Lullabies or simple, calm melodies work well for this exercise.

- Align your body

- Now, as you are holding a peaceful image in your mind (maybe a favorite place in nature or another comforting image), hum this melody to yourself, softly. Do not use the words yet!

- If any part of the song feels too high or too low, adjust your beginning note until it feels just right.

- As you hum, with your lips closed, try to feel inside your mouth and throat as if you were singing an open 'ah': enjoy this space inside your mouth and throat.

- Now add a subtle, genuine inner smile to your hum. Observe how smiling like that feels like the sun breaking through the clouds! This kind of smile may or may not be noticeable around your mouth – it bubbles up from your belly and comes primarily through the eyes. It "lights up" your face.

- Imagine humming to a baby with that smile.

- Try to add elements from the previous exercises

without losing that inner smile: unlock your knees; move your belly; breathe in by creating space and relaxing; let your tones slide gently from one tone to the next rather than experiencing them as separate.

- Switch from humming to the NG sound. "Hum" the song with this NG. Smile! Listen!

- Now practice to open your mouth gently, so you look like you are singing "Ah" *without* releasing the NG.

- Try other sounds: oooh, oh, ah (in that order!)

- Now sing the song with words: is it easier or harder now for you to sing the song beautifully?

- Try another song, going through the same process.

Things to observe:

- Is my voice cutting out at times? Allow more air and energy to travel through your generous space in your throat. Turn your "inner smile meter" up another notch. In other words: raise your vibration!

- Is my voice tight? Allow more movement in your imagination and in your body. You might need to change your mental image to something more fluid, like a river, a fountain or an ocean. Relax your jaw. Even more.

- What kind of feelings show up in connection to this song? Acknowledge them but don't give them much attention. You can always smile about that later. Keep your primary focus on your technique, on the image in your mind and your sound quality.

How to choose a teacher

*

How do you know if you are doing the exercises right?

*

Well, you really don't, unless you have an experienced teacher to help you with his/her ears and eyes. Learning how to sing from a book is as impossible as learning how to drive a car from a book. Without the experienced driver to guide the beginner, it would all remain purely hypothetical. But how can we go about finding the right teacher?
Aside from the obvious practical considerations like recommendations, distance and transportation, scheduling logistics and cost, there are other elements to pay attention to.
  Singing teachers' approaches are as different as the styles of music they offer, their career agendas or the cultural backgrounds they come from. Ask yourself: what do I want to learn this for? If you want to become an opera singer, you don't want to work with someone who specializes in pop-style; if you want to sing Jazz, you may not want to study with a traditional opera school; if you simply want to learn how to carry a tune, you don't want to stress yourself with an ambitious teacher who likes to showcase his/her students in recitals.
  Once you have found some possible instructors, ask these available teachers some questions. Maybe, with the permission

of the other student, you can observe someone else's lesson to get an idea of the teacher's skills and his/her way of relating to the student.

Make sure you feel comfortable in the teacher's presence. If you are in any way anxious, fearful, irritated or otherwise uncomfortable with the teacher's personality, your negative emotional state will severely interfere with your learning process.

Also aim to find out what his/her general goal is for the students and look for possible red flags.

Good Signs:	Red Flags:
The teacher is committed to designing individual approaches, depending on each student's ability and motivation	The teacher works with a one-size-fits-all method and timeline
The teacher is patient, focused and humorous	The teacher is impatient and/or distracted
The basic insight "everyone can learn how to sing" is a foundation for the teacher's work	"Some people should not even try to sing" is part of the teacher's method of selecting his/her students
The teacher can accurately explain and demonstrate exercises and techniques.	The teacher avoids demonstrating, or his/her demonstrations do not seem to accurately match the explanation given.

Conclusion

This little collection of thoughts, insights and bits of information was meant to encourage and inspire further study, and I hope I have succeeded in sparking your interest. My small list of further reading suggestions at the end can help you continue on from here.

While there are obviously enormous forces in play that exert every effort to prevent humanity from evolving, there are equal or even more powerful forces accessible to us now that can propel us into new, unprecedented levels of consciousness. Where there are deep shadows there is great light!
Many of the tools we are given by divine wisdom to access, spread and benefit from these newly accessible light-forces, are surprisingly simple. Singing well is one of them.

I strive to be awake and aware of, but never focus much on, the forces that suppress our own creative process, our own independent thoughts, our own sounds, our own images, our food and especially our ability to communicate directly with our fellow human beings. Instead, I aim to focus my spiritual spotlights directly on our *new spiritual capacities* and become ever more creative in finding new ways to develop them. Study and cultivation of the human 'sound-system' and its impact on communication and social awareness is one of my main approaches to this task.

Human interaction with true interest, compassionate communication, non-judgment, spiritual validation, humanitarian outreach, non-competitive work and play, universal joy and global empathy and cooperation are all essential human capacities necessary for our survival on this planet.

Practical involvement in music and art in all forms (from singing and playing instruments to painting and drawing, to sculpture, architecture, film, literature, holistic education, organic farming and gardening) fosters these human capacities. I strive therefore to facilitate the renewed connection of humanity to music and the arts in all forms. I will continue to search out ways to learn and perfect more and more of these capacities.

It has become my task to teach my fellow human beings how to cultivate silence, to listen and observe with care and to develop an attentive, compassionate awareness of others. My primary approach to these objectives is the study and cultivation of the human singing voice. I teach my students to find interest in and compassion for everyone around us. Holistic and conscious singing is a shortcut to these human capacities.

Please come and sing with me some day!

Bibliography

and Additional Recommended Reading

(in alphabetical order)

Campbell, Don. *The Mozart Effect: Tapping the power of Music to Heal the Body, Strengthen the Mind and Unlock the Spirit.* (Avon Books Inc.)

A powerful testimony of the effects of music on our whole being from a healer and educator. Campbell supports his work with scientific studies and research and practical examples of clients, students, musicians and therapists.

Goldman, Jonathan. *Healing Sounds: the Power of Harmonics.* (Healing Arts Press, Rochester, Vermont)

Goldberg's book is a more esoteric, deeper and more thorough rendition of what Campbell has attempted to do: to show, through the laws of physics and esoteric teachings the healing power of music.

Hicks, Esther and Jerry. *Ask and it is Given: Learning to Manifest your Desires.* (Hay House publications)

This is not a book about music. It is, however, one of the more useful New Age books that teaches us about the power of positive thinking, which in my experience is essential for developing an effortless, healthy singing voice.

Mathieu, W.A., *The Listening Book: Discovering your own Music*. (Shambhala Publications Inc.)

Very poetic and meditative prose, this book is a muse for the searching soul. It encourages finding one's own music, fine-tuning one's listening and searching out new perspectives in the field of sound and music.

Powell, John. *How Music Works*: *The Science and Psychology of Beautiful Sounds, From Beethoven to The Beatles and Beyond.* (Little Brown and Company, Hachette Book Group)

This is a highly entertaining and vastly informative book. This British author could be a standup comedian! Powell's writing style is accessible and witty. He is able to make the most mathematical physics phenomena look easy and fun. He answers questions about an enormous list of common musical elements and also very particular, scientific questions about music. From the absolute basics to finicky details from the world of acoustics, Powell explains everything you want to know and some things you have never considered asking about. He uses fairly simple vocabulary and takes nothing for granted. This book is a very useful companion for trained musicians, scientists, teachers and anyone else curious about the how and why of music.

Godwin, Joscelyn (editor). *Cosmic Music: Musical Keys to the Interpretation of Reality.* (Inner Traditions, Rochester, Vermont)

This is a book from the Anthroposophical stream of thought and scientific research. This collection of six essays by three different authors is a somewhat cerebral celebration of Science, culture and esoteric philosophy, dealing with harmonics, planetary and natural frequencies and significant turning points in history from a musical perspective.

Rosenberg, Marshall B., Ph.D. *Nonviolent Communication: A Language of Life*. (Puddledancer Press)

This is a practical guide to developing awareness and skill in HOW we meet and communicate with our fellow human beings, celebrating the fact that a non-violent approach to a difference in opinion can magically melt away resentment, misunderstanding and conflict.
   Although Rosenberg does not speak about music, his work is nonetheless a very important piece of my approach to singing.

Steiner, Rudolf. *The Inner Nature of Music and the Experience of Tone:* Selected Lectures from the work of Rudolf Steiner, GA 283. (Anthroposophic Press). Translated from the German by Maria St. Goar and edited by Alice Wulsin.
Originally published as: *Das Wesen des Musikalischen und das Tonerlebnis im Menschen,* (Rudolf Steiner Verlag, Dornach). Also previously published under the title: *The Essence of Music and the Experience of Tone.*

If you are willing to explore esoteric depths of the human condition and its connection to music and you don't mind reading difficult books, this treasure is for you.

Tamura, Michael. *You are the Answer: Discovering and Fulfilling your Soul Purpose.* (Llewellyn Publications)

Not many books I have come across are as empowering and helpful as this one in the field of inner growth, awareness and the development of new capacities. Michael firmly and playfully puts the responsibility for your biography, for your happiness and success back into your own, creative hands.

   Michael Tamura is one of my mentors. He is a spiritual teacher, healer and clairvoyant, but he is also a musician: he plays music, loves to sing and write songs. He has encouraged me many times to share my gift of song with the world. Although his book is not about music, it has a musical feel to it, like a good composition, that has made it quite enjoyable and accessible to me. His "spiritual toolkit" at the end of his book is a great beginning to developing awareness of energy flow through and around our body and to shaping and holding clear images in our minds, all very important elements to a holistic singing approach.

Werbeck-Svärdström , Valborg. *The School of Uncovering the Voice: The cleansing Power of Song* (Sophia Books Rudolf Steiner press 2002).
 Original German title: Die Schule der Stimmenthüllung, Verlag am Goetheanum 1969)
This book is not an easy one to read, but it is a true gem in the world of professional vocal work. It has provided me with invaluable insights and helped me formulate new questions in my search for a deeper understanding. This book is the basis, the "text book" if you will, for the schooling I have completed and am certified for. I have read it several times and will probably return

to it for several more reviews. It is so full of deep insights and esoteric connections that it can be either incredibly inspiring or intensely bewildering. I strongly recommend some committed vocal studies *before* venturing into this book.

Wooten, Victor L. *The Music Lesson: A Spiritual Search for Growth Through Music.* (Berkley Trade)
This book is a fictional story of finding oneself, finding one's own voice through music studies, while providing plenty of information and answers to basic elements of music and musicianship.

A Few Websites:
If you are not familiar with Waldorf Education, you may want to explore the following website, where you can find many articles and helpful links about this approach to educating the whole human being:
www.whywaldorfworks.org

http://waldorfmusic.org This is the website of AWME (Association for Waldorf Music Education) is a wonderful support system for music teachers and has, besides interesting articles, a great list of valuable resources for bringing music into the classroom.

The following organizations were mentioned in my book. Here they are once again:

www.epa.gov (Environmental Protection Agency)

www.gcaudio.com (Galen Carol Audio)

www.cdc.gov/niosh (Center for Disease Control and Prevention/ National Institute for Occupational Safety and Health)

http://www.asha.org/ (American Speech-Language-Hearing Association)

http://www.healingsounds.com (Johnathan Goldman)

About the Author

Eva Cranstoun (born in Vienna, Austria in 1971) has been singing and practicing live music and performing arts her whole life. Her angelic voice and effective teaching style have moved hundreds and have inspired a great number of students and course participants to continue their studies with her. The psychological and spiritual aspects of the human voice, as well as its impact on our general well being have been a constant topic of study throughout her adult life. She is certified as instructor and therapist of the *School of Uncovering the Voice* (European holistic approach to vocal development) and holds a diploma in Waldorf Education. As vocal performer, experienced Waldorf educator and therapist, Eva has acquired a wide perspective and deep soul-understanding of the human voice. She is married and lives in Fair Oaks, California with her husband William and three children.

www.ingramcontent.com/pod-product-compliance
Lightning Source LLC
Chambersburg PA
CBHW061329040426
42444CB00011B/2828